What Your Collea

You need to buy two copies of this book, [...] [...] on your desk so you can grab it when you need immediate strategies to handle the challenges that arise. The other to keep on your bedside table so you can read it again for comfort, reassurance, and encouragement. This is the book that will keep you in education . . . sane, calm, competent, and resilient.

—Roselind Wiseman
Co-founder of Cultures of Dignity
Boulder, CO

This new edition is hardcore. Newly updated with their characteristic humor, real classroom examples, robust new research, action steps, and appendices worth the price alone, Debbie and Jack have outdone themselves. This is real aloe on the wounds and a bright lantern for the way forward to converting radical hope into effective educational practice while finding grounds for joy along the way.

—Rick Wormeli
Teacher/Principal Training and Author
Herdon, VA

With *Deliberate Optimism* you will have everything you need to reimagine an environment of passion and purpose. It is an essential guide for achieving the best version of yourself! Every teacher and district team member should be given this book to help them accelerate kindness and caring in our schools.

—Martinrex Kedziora, Superintendent of Schools
Moreno Valley Unified School District
Moreno Valley, CA

This book serves as a beacon of hope. We sail forward guided by the positive momentum of these Principles and Action Steps to navigate the present challenges and prepare for those to come. Get on board for a joyful journey of deliberate optimism based on honesty, humor, and hope.

—Stephen Sroka, National Teacher Hall of Fame Inductee
Walt Disney American Teacher of the Year
Fellow of the American School Health Association and
Adjunct Assistant Professor, School of Medicine,
Case Western Reserve University
Cleveland, OH

PRAISE FOR THE FIRST EDITION

This book reminds us that we have far more control than we realize. The message of *Deliberate Optimism* reinforces my personal coping strategy of humming "Keep on the Sunny Side" when I encounter negativity and challenges!

—Deborah Kasak, Executive Director,
National Forum to Accelerate Middle-Grades
Reform Schools to Watch Initiative

Deliberate Optimism is for all of those teachers who got into education because of a love for children and a passion for learning. Read this book . . . and regain your optimism.

—Peter DeWitt, Independent Consultant,
Finding Common Ground by *Education Week*,
Corwin Author, and Consulting Editor for the
Corwin Connected Educators Series

Sometimes teachers forget that taking care of ourselves is an important part of the job. *Deliberate Optimism* helps educators learn how refill our mental and emotional gas tanks—or at least increase our fuel efficiency.

—Roxanna Elden, Author, *See Me After Class:
Advice for Teachers by Teachers*

Every district leader and building principal should put this book in the hands of teachers and teacher assistants—and then model the kind of deliberate optimism teachers have a right to expect from their leaders.

—Ron Nash, Presenter and Author of
The Active Classroom series

This book is a must-have resource. Easy to read and implement, it offers a wealth of sensible, realistic, and inspiring advice about how to successfully manage the daily business of being a classroom teacher. Its positive message is simply empowering!

—Julia G. Thompson, Author, *The First-Year
Teacher's Survival Guide*

Not only is the book a singular call to arms for teachers to reclaim their joy, but within these pages are real strategies for healing our souls and growing positive, nurturing classrooms.

—Kevin Honeycutt, International Speaker, Author,
Song Writer, and Program Developer, Educational Services and
Staff Development Association of Central Kansas

This book provides a framework for taking responsibility in classrooms, choosing to see the positives, dealing with problems rather than dwelling on them, recognizing that choices are always available, and building relationships with all in the school community.

—Charla Buford Bunker, Literacy Specialist
Great Falls High School, MT

deliberate
OPTIMISM

2ND EDITION

*This book is dedicated to our families and friends
who support us unconditionally and to our fellow educators
who still believe that what they do matters.*

DEBBIE SILVER • JACK C. BERCKEMEYER

deliberate
OPTIMISM
2ND EDITION

STILL RECLAIMING THE
JOY IN EDUCATION

CORWIN

FOR INFORMATION:

Corwin

A SAGE Company

2455 Teller Road

Thousand Oaks, California 91320

(800) 233-9936

www.corwin.com

SAGE Publications Ltd.

1 Oliver's Yard

55 City Road

London EC1Y 1SP

United Kingdom

SAGE Publications India Pvt. Ltd.

Unit No 323-333, Third Floor, F-Block

International Trade Tower Nehru Place

New Delhi 110 019

SAGE Publications Asia-Pacific Pte. Ltd.

18 Cross Street #10-10/11/12

China Square Central

Singapore 048423

President: Mike Soules

Vice President and
  Editorial Director: Monica Eckman

Senior Acquisitions Editor: Tanya Ghans

Content Development
  Manager: Desirée A. Bartlett

Editorial Assistant: Nyle De Leon

Production Editor: Amy Schroller

Copy Editor: Karin Rathert

Typesetter: C&M Digitals (P) Ltd.

Cover Designer: Rose Storey

Marketing Manager: Morgan Fox

Printed in the United States of America

Library of Congress Control Number: 2023935912

This book is printed on acid-free paper.

23 24 25 26 27 10 9 8 7 6 5 4 3 2

CONTENTS

PREFACE

*Your profession is not what brings home your
weekly paycheck, your profession is what you're
put here on earth to do, with such passion and such
intensity that it becomes spiritual in calling.*

—Vincent van Gogh

In 2015, we (Debbie and Jack), along with our friend and colleague, Judith Baenen, published *Deliberate Optimism: Reclaiming the Joy in Education* in response to our work with teachers and leaders who reported a distressing decline in their feelings of work-related status and power. A general sensation of helplessness and futility seemed to be growing among educators as the public perception of schools reached new lows. The escalating focus on standardized curriculums and assessments, increasingly overbearing teacher evaluations, growing breakdown in parental support, and other factors gave rise to a lost sense of enthusiasm for and joy in working in education.

Our purpose was to write a book that discussed the existing challenges facing educators and provide reasonable, effective ways to restore efficacy to all the adults who act as advocates for students in schools. We added humor because, well, that's just who we are. After the book's publication, we traveled the country and abroad helping teachers and leaders rethink how to empower themselves and reclaim their optimism, even during challenging circumstances. We felt we were successful in assisting fellow educators reduce rising anxiety by laughing more and learning not to fret over circumstances beyond their control.

Then March 2020 brought on more challenges than any of us could have anticipated. The exigent burdens on school systems and individuals beginning with the first shelter-in-place orders through the present have driven teacher job satisfaction to an all-time low.

Unfortunately, the added strain generated by the pandemic, divisive political and cultural debates, and even greater distrust from parents triggered many in education to question their *calling*. Education already had attrition problems before the pandemic, and now the resultant toxic levels of stress have teachers leaving the profession in numbers never seen before.

Despite the growing unrest and increasing anxiety levels, we (the authors) are adamant about buoying current educators and encouraging positive, effective people to join the ranks of those of us who still believe we can make significant differences for learners. We maintain that teaching remains the most noble profession. What other group of people has more ability to shape the future by empowering the next generation to think, to create, and to act compassionately toward their fellow humans?

We do not mean to imply that there are no longer "pockets of excellence" across the nation where both students and teachers embrace their learning institutions as places that are safe, engaging, and generally happy. All of us can point to schools that offer the best kinds of learning environments for students and are appreciated by the adults who work there as well as the communities they serve. We hope that every school is working to grow toward that kind of quality.

Because exemplary schools are not universal, however, there are policy makers, community members, administrators, parents, and even teachers who have allowed themselves to get caught in the *blame game* in which pointing fingers gets priority over working on solutions. And because most of the pointed fingers of late have been directed at classrooms, some teachers quite understandably have taken a defensive posture as well as defeatist attitude. This negativity helps no one, and as we like to say, "We are done with that!"

Together Debbie and Jack decided to revise this book to include even more information about how we as educators can take back our power, our joy, and our optimism. For every teacher, the journey to this profession is a complex and unique road. We believe the incredible adventure of teaching is indeed a calling, and it requires ongoing purpose and effort to sustain its viability. We authors grew up in different parts of the country, taught in vastly diverse school settings, and we each have our own areas of expertise. Nonetheless, we have been friends and colleagues for almost three decades, and we share a common belief that a sense of humor, an awareness of personal responsibility, a commitment to purpose, and a feeling of realistic optimism are the keys to sustained fulfillment in this profession.

You won't find suggestions that promote what many are calling "toxic positivity" in these pages. We know first-hand that educators are worn out and overwhelmed. Some are uncertain about their effectiveness as they question their purpose. And amid the self-doubt and anxiety about the state of education, they have been bombarded with admonitions to silence their negative emotions, deny their anguish, and at least pretend that everything is okay.

Deliberate Optimism, Second Edition: Still Reclaiming the Joy in Education provides an updated look at how now more than ever teachers and leaders must acknowledge and seek to resolve the unsustainable stress levels on all those connected with schooling. It provides a realistic view of how individuals and teams can empower themselves and each other to create solutions that restore teacher autonomy, competence, and relevance, thus reigniting a sense of hope and purpose in our profession.

The Revised Principles of Deliberate Optimism for Educators

We think there are some concrete practical steps that will help leaders and teachers remain hopeful no matter what the adversity. Influenced by the works of some of the world's greatest optimists, Dale Carnegie, Norman Vincent Peale, Martin Seligman, Stephen Covey, and others, we originally developed five principles for deliberate optimism. With the input of educators across the country, particularly Urbandale Community School District in Iowa, we have revised what are now our *Four Principles for Deliberate Optimism for Educators*. We use these throughout this book to guide the discussion about how teachers, administrators, and other staff can intentionally and effectively become realistic optimists.

Four Principles for Deliberate Optimism for Educators

1. Gather information.

2. Control what you can.

3. Do something positive.

4. Own your part.

Each chapter covers a different aspect of maintaining optimism in an educational setting. Through research-based strategies, practical examples, action steps, and thought-provoking scenarios, the authors provide food for thought along with enough humor to make the journey fun. General Discussion Questions and Action Steps for Leaders follow each chapter, and an appendix of further activities is provided at the end of the book.

ESSENTIALS FOR HAPPINESS

- Something to love

- Something to do

- Something to hope for

—Author unknown

Introduction—*Choosing to Enter Education Is a Telling Vote for Optimism*—discusses the meaning of optimism and its component parts (joy, positivity, happiness, hope) and why it is an essential element in education. The dangers of "toxic positivity" are compared to the benefits of realistic optimism.

Chapter 1—*Principle #1: Gather Information*—encourages educators to find authentic answers by going as directly to the source as possible. Suggestions are provided about how to filter our perception of the motives of others.

Chapter 2—*Principle #2: Control What You Can*—explores how self-efficacy is enhanced by determining what we can control and by focusing our efforts on the controllable elements in our lives. Through "disputation theory" and "reframing," we can feel more energized and negate being debilitated by feelings of helplessness.

Chapter 3—*Principle #3: Do Something Positive*—points out ways that action can rejuvenate us as it creates helpful momentum. Proactive action steps for maintaining one's health give educators specific strategies for building personal resiliency.

Chapter 4—*Principle #4: Own Your Part*—explores the idea of educators "taking back our power" through collegial feedback and support. Practical steps for promoting "radical responsibility" among staff members are examined.

Chapter 5—*Mental Health Is Health*—argues that without mental health, there can be no real health. This chapter offers several positive ideas for meeting the mental health needs of the adults at school as well as providing steps individuals can take on their own.

Chapter 6—*"But We Have This* ONE *Teacher Who Keeps Ruining Everything!"*—examines extrovert/introvert tendencies and generational differences to help better understand ourselves and how we can interact more positively with colleagues. It also offers tips on minimizing the effect of negative associates as well as bullies.

Chapter 7—*Building a Positive Shared School Community*—focuses on intentionally building supportive relationships among leaders, staff, and students. Specific social-emotional learning activities geared at enhancing trust and cooperation are described and discussed.

Chapter 8—*Joyful School Communities—The Sum of Their Parts*—looks at what teachers, leaders, parents/caretakers, and local communities can do to help restore optimism and hope in our nation's schools. Ideas and activities for building camaraderie throughout the community are provided.

What's New in This Edition

- Additional focus on leadership for both teachers and administrators

- Updated information and suggestions addressing major changes in education since the 2015 first edition

- Revised, succinct Principles of Optimism

- Chapters revised to include a designated chapter for each Principle of Optimism

- Interactive "Action Step" exercises for the reader in each chapter

- Updated research and examples

- QR codes in every chapter for additional resources

- Added chapter on mental health

- More General Discussion Questions and Action Steps for School Leaders at the end of each chapter

This Book Will Help You . . .

- Be able to employ purposeful, intentional strategies to maintain a sense of optimism about your work

- Understand the importance of maintaining one's sense of self as well as one's health

- Receive valuable insights on dealing with differing and/or difficult people in the profession

- Obtain valuable ideas for fostering positive school relationships

- Evaluate how to positively interact with those outside the school setting to build a shared community

To sum it up, teachers are expected to cheerfully address standards-based instruction (SBI) and other Common Core curriculum (CC) with appropriate response to intervention (RTI) techniques while including problem-based learning (PBL) and end-of-course-assessment (EOC). They should use positive behavior intervention and supports (PBIS) to ensure student engagement and create behavior intervention plans (BIPs) for students who don't wish to comply. They must learn to separate student data gleaned from standardized tests that comply with the Every Student Succeeds Act (ESSA) and discuss the results in their professional learning communities (PLCs) as part of their ongoing professional development (PD). At the same time, they are expected to design plans for differentiated instruction (DI) utilizing each child's multiple intelligences (MI) while writing individual education programs (IEPs) for students who need additional support. All this must be done with an eye toward a gradual release of responsibility (GRR) so that no child is left behind (NCLB). (Perhaps not ironically, we are witnessing the current trend of *Rising Exasperation Towards Impractical, Restrictive Edicts* [RETIRE]).

Seriously, we are concerned with new surveys indicating as many as 44 percent of current teachers will leave the profession in the next two years (Merrimack College, 2022), and 42 percent of principals across the country reported the pandemic has accelerated their plans to leave the profession (Levin et al., 2020). Educators now lead the latest *Gallup Panel Workforce Study* reporting the highest burnout rate (52%) among all U.S. workers (Marken & Agrawal, 2022). Nevertheless, we believe there are many steps leaders and educators can take to alleviate some of the basic annoyances as well as the overt and covert challenges educators face daily.

In *Deliberate Optimism, Second Edition: Still Trying to Reclaim the Joy in Education*, we endeavor to help school leaders and their teachers regain a sense power and influence. We believe that a candid examination of how we educators are sometimes our own worst enemy will help us as a group to stop shooting ourselves in the foot and start speaking in a collective voice that will be heard. We want our profession to regain its moral calling and educators to reclaim their joy in doing their jobs.

We respectfully (and sometimes tongue-in-cheek) submit our ideas for our brothers and sisters in the *educationnation.*

Debbie Silver

Jack Berckemeyer

ACKNOWLEDGMENTS

Thanks to my friend and colleague Jack Berckemeyer and my friend and former collaborator on the first edition of the book Judith Baenen. You two continue to inspire me with you unwavering support of kids, of middle-level education, and of me. I know my life if better because you are in it.

—Debbie Silver

A special thanks to my friends and "partners in crime," Debbie Silver and Judith Baenen. Thanks also to Lawrence Silver for his patience as Debbie worked long hours on our book. Together we help each other find our own *deliberate optimism*.

—Jack Berckemeyer

We are most appreciative of the support we have had from Corwin, particularly, Desirée Bartlett, Tanya Ghans, Karin Rathert, and Nyle DeLeon. You made this revision possible and the journey a lot easier.

—Debbie and Jack

ABOUT THE AUTHORS

Debbie Silver is a humorist, consultant, and retired educator with over thirty years of experience as a classroom teacher, staff development facilitator, and university professor. As a classroom teacher, Dr. Silver won numerous awards, including the *1990 Louisiana Teacher of the Year* award. She speaks worldwide on issues involving education and is a passionate advocate for students and teachers.

Debbie wrote the best-selling books *Drumming to the Beat of Different Marchers* and *Fall Down 7 Times, Get Up 8*. She co-wrote the best-selling *Teaching Kids to Thrive*. In 1990, Debbie Pace and Lawrence Silver merged their families of three boys (Debbie) and two boys (Lawrence) as they married and eventually both earned their doctorate degrees (to form a "pair-a-docs"). They currently reside in Melissa, Texas.

One of the nation's most popular keynote speakers and professional development presenters, Debbie has given presentations around the world (including 49 states [Hey, Delaware, let's talk!], Canada, Mexico, Europe, the Middle East, Australia, Africa, and Asia), helping audiences to interact with students on a more meaningful level.

While inspiring educators to enjoy the job they once loved, she reminds them of how important they are in the lives of children, their families, and the world. Through her writing and her speaking, she makes essential points while sharing poignant stories and lots of laughs.

Jack Berckemeyer is a nationally recognized presenter, author, and humorist, Jack Berckemeyer began his career as a middle school teacher in Denver, Colorado. After only two years, he was recognized as the outstanding educator at his school and in his district. Then in 2003, Jack received the Outstanding Alumni Award from the Falcon School District. Jack has also served as a judge for the Disney American Teacher Awards and has served on the selection committee for the USA TODAY All-Teacher Team. Jack has a master's degree in middle level education as well as an administrator's degree.

For 13 years, Jack served as the assistant executive director for the National Middle School Association. He is the owner of Berckemeyer Consulting Group, where he has presented in hundreds of school districts and conference settings both nationally and internationally.

Jack is known not only for his keynotes and workshops but is also highly regarded as one of the best long-term professional developers in the country. Jack is best-practice focused and research based. He is in high demand and enjoys working with districts that truly want to see measurable changes. As the owner and director of *NUTS and BOLTS—The Never Boring Conference for Educators*, Jack brings conferences for educators to a whole new level of engagement by focusing on best practices and offering realistic and practical hands-on tools to increase success for educators, schools, and students.

He is the author of *Managing the Madness: A Practical Guide to Middle Grades Classrooms; Taming of the Team: How Great Teams Work Together; How to Do Virtual Teaching Even If You Have a Face for Radio;* and numerous educational articles. In addition, he is the lead author of the comprehensive professional development curriculum: *Elements of Effective Teaming.* Jack has also co-authored *Deliberate Optimism: Reclaiming the Joy in Education* (with Debbie Silver and Judith Baenen); *The What, Why, and How of Student-Led Conferences* (with Patti Kinney), and *H.E.L.P. for Teachers* (with Judith Baenen). His latest book, *Successful Middle School Teaming,* was released fall of 2022 and is the companion guide to *The Successful Middle School: This We Believe.*

Jack lives in Denver, Colorado, and has no pets or plants.

INTRODUCTION

CHOOSING TO ENTER EDUCATION IS A TELLING VOTE FOR OPTIMISM

Optimism is the foundation of all good teaching. Optimism in the face of daunting reality is downright heroic—and that, in fact, is what good teachers practice all day long while others denigrate their contributions to society.

—Rafe Esquith

Who Chooses Education as a Profession?

There are probably as many paths to teaching as there are teachers. Maybe you always knew you were going to be a teacher. As a child, you spent hours in your room preparing lessons and delivering them to captive younger siblings or to Max, the aging family dog. You loved dry erase boards, markers, and stickers. Perhaps your parents were teachers, and you quite naturally fell into the familiar profession. Or maybe early on you learned the joy of teaching another person something they did not know before.

Possibly you were the dispassionate learner who never really entered the conversations at school and could not figure out why the kids on the front row were so excited. You did just enough to get by and prayed that everyone, especially your teachers, would leave you alone. Then later in life, you decided you would like to be the person to reach out to other outliers and to make ever learner feel a part of the school community.

And of course, some of our greatest teachers freely admit they were their own teachers' worst nightmare. (Nothing warms our hearts like watching a former troublesome student become a teacher—especially if they are assigned several students who act just like they did.) Rule-breaking-back-talking-defiant-attitude students often grow up and want to go back as teachers so they can change a system they feel failed them. Whatever the path that got us here, we joined this profession because we believed we could make this world a better place—one student at a time.

When we decided to become teachers, we entered an unbreakable pact with the future. We promised to do the best we could with what we had and what we knew to successfully mold the next generation. As educators, we know that it is our obligation to grow, to learn, and to reflect on how to improve ourselves every year so that we leave the future of this world in the best, most capable, most educated hands imaginable. If we don't subscribe to this noble purpose, then what are we doing in education?

Why Is Optimism So Important for Educators?

When we (the authors) write about optimism, we do not intend to imply that teachers should show up every day with fake grins pasted on their faces. Nor are we talking about educators doing cartwheels of joy down the hall to face an angry parent in the office, dancing gleefully into a required professional development meeting on blood-borne pathogens, or squealing with delight when given the task of disaggregating student data from the latest high sweepstakes test results. Just as with any job or profession, we all have duties that are less than pleasant. Our intent is to examine realistic, purposeful strategies teachers and school leaders can employ to restore their hope in a system they feel is rapidly heading off course.

We realize the challenges of teaching today are greater than they have ever been before. Schools have become a political minefield of mandated policies and procedures that censure original thinking and creative innovation. Schools are experiencing both academic and emotional deficits. Staff shortages are widespread while those who are there must deal with the pain of families who suffered trauma and fallout from the COVID pandemic. In the court of social media, schools are suffering the downward slide of public opinion. Grace, patience, trust, gratitude, and empathy seem to be in short supply among both school employees and student families. As NASSP's 2015 principal of the year writes, "We are not okay" (Meade, 2022).

Action Step I.1

FIND YOUR BASELINE OPTIMISM SCORE

Before you get started, you may want to get a baseline score on your overall optimism ranking on the *Los Angeles Times* **Optimism Test,** which you can access by scanning QR Code I.1. Did the results surprise you or confirm what you already knew? See also Appendix I.2. You can also explore your current life orientation toward optimism with the short test in Appendix I.1.

What Is Optimism?

Is *optimism* a product of nature or nurture? We believe that one's disposition may be influenced by nature, but a state of optimism can be developed and maintained by anyone who chooses to frame their perceptions in a manner that is both realistic and positive.

There are those who believe that people are either born with optimistic tendencies or they are not. Some people are told, "You have always been a happy person. Even as a baby, you were such a cheerful little thing." Or a person might overhear a parent say, "He was a cranky, finicky infant, and he hasn't changed a bit. It's like living with Oscar the Grouch. He could find a way to depress Tony Robbins." Perhaps you know a student or an adult whose natural facial expression is a frown. Maybe you attribute this negative persona to something within the person that cannot be changed. We do not agree. There is a reason we like to use the term *deliberate optimism.* We believe optimism can be learned, developed, and maintained. We do acknowledge that some people seem to be more outwardly cheerful than others, but we strongly argue that anyone can deliberately change their attitude.

Optimism is sometimes used synonymously with *hopefulness, joy, happiness,* and *positivity.* We want to clarify that what we are encouraging is called *realistic optimism,* which encompasses each of these terms listed. A single-minded optimist in a Jurassic Park movie might say, "Yeah, I knew those dinosaurs wouldn't get me. I never doubted I'd get out alive. I just live a charmed life." A realistic optimist would say, "Wow, that was a close call, and here's what I'd do differently next time . . ." Realistic optimists recognize the negative, work to fix the fixable (accepting, coping with, or deemphasizing the unfixable), and intentionally focus their attention and energy on solutions.

In the broadest sense, optimism generally refers to looking on the bright side of virtually everything (i.e., "Yes, the pandemic was challenging, but think how it is going to help us improve education. It's really been a blessing in disguise."). On the other hand, *pessimism* generally refers to assuming the worst possible outcome about everything (i.e., "The pandemic was the tipping point of the collapse of public education. It's all going to be downhill from here. Count me out."). Seldom is anyone totally optimistic or pessimistic, and even optimism needs some parameters.

We are not asking educators to be dogged optimists. An unequivocal optimist may have a totally unrealistic hope for a better outcome. The attitude of "I'm just going to trust the universe" could negate any requirement for personal action or responsibility. Possible pitfalls can be overlooked as well as missing opportunities for change and growth. Studies have shown that too much optimism can lead to disappointment and loss of hope.

The Stockdale Paradox

Jim Collins, author of *Good to Great*, describes a negative consequence of blind optimism. He writes about a powerful psychological duality of maintaining unwavering faith in the endgame while accepting brutal facts. He calls this the *Stockdale Paradox*.

> The name refers to Admiral Jim Stockdale, who was the highest-ranking United States military officer in the "Hanoi Hilton" prisoner-of-war camp during the height of the Vietnam War. Tortured over twenty times during his eight-year imprisonment from 1965 to 1973, Stockdale lived out the war without any prisoner's rights, no set release date, and no certainty as to whether he would even survive to see his family again.

> As I [Jim Collins] moved through the book [*In Love and War*, written by Stockdale and his wife], I found myself getting depressed. It just seemed so bleak—the uncertainty of his fate, the brutality of his captors, and so forth. And then, it dawned on me: "Here I am sitting in my warm and comfortable office, looking out over the beautiful Stanford campus on a beautiful Saturday afternoon. I'm getting depressed reading this, and I know the end of the story! I know that he gets out, reunites

with his family, becomes a national hero, and gets to spend the later years of his life studying philosophy on this same beautiful campus. If it feels depressing for me, how on earth did he deal with it when he was actually there and *did not know the end of the story?*"

"I never lost faith in the end of the story," he said, when I asked him. "I never doubted not only that I would get out, but also that I would prevail in the end and turn the experience into the defining event of my life, which, in retrospect, I would not trade."

I didn't say anything for many minutes, and we continued the slow walk toward the faculty club, Stockdale limping and arc-swinging his stiff leg that had never fully recovered from repeated torture. Finally, after about a hundred meters of silence, I asked, "Who didn't make it out?"

"Oh, that's easy," he said. "The optimists."

"The optimists? I don't understand," I said, now completely confused, given what he'd said a hundred meters earlier.

"The optimists. Oh, they were the ones who said, 'We're going to be out by Christmas.' And Christmas would come, and Christmas would go. Then they'd say, 'We're going to be out by Easter.' And Easter would come, and Easter would go. And then Thanksgiving, and then it would be Christmas again. And they died of a broken heart."

Another long pause, and more walking. Then he turned to me and said, "This is a very important lesson. You must never confuse faith that you will prevail in the end—which you can never afford to lose—with the discipline to confront the most brutal facts of your current reality, whatever they might be."

To this day, I carry a mental image of Stockdale admonishing the optimists: "We're not getting out by Christmas; deal with it!" (Collins, 2001, pp. 83–85)

We educators do not yet know the end of our story either. We must focus on what's currently working in our situations and take what steps we can take to make things better. We can't afford to ignore problems or presume that fate will always turn in our favor. We need to prepare ourselves to face the tough situations we now have and form a plan of action not only to cope with but to thrive in these difficult times. There are problems in education; let's deal with them!

> *I am fundamentally an optimist. Whether that comes from nature or nurture, I cannot say. Part of being optimistic is keeping one's head pointed toward the sun, one's feet moving forward. There were many dark moments when my faith in humanity was sorely tested, but I would not and could not give myself up to despair. That way lays defeat and death.*
>
> —Nelson Mandela, *Long Walk to Freedom: Autobiography of Nelson Mandela*

Optimism and Hope

Obviously, while Admiral Stockdale prepared for the worst, he never gave up hope. Part of realistic optimism requires that we educators continue to believe that our schools can work and what we do improves the lives of children. *Hope* is the belief that our future can be better than our past and that we have a role to play in making that future a reality. Just as we think hope is giving every learner a *reasonable* chance at success, we believe teachers and leaders deserve a system that provides them a sufficient chance to be successful. We explore this concept further in later chapters.

Upon the retirement of thirty-five-year veteran kindergarten teacher Lil Lufkin, her head of school at Calhoun School in Manhattan, Nelson (2013), wrote the following tribute letter:

Dear Lil,

Thirty-five years, 15 kids—give or take—to a class. That makes 525 kids you have loved and taught. You've spent about 50,400 hours teaching during those 35 years. That's enough time to visit Pluto and return, yet you have stayed in one place. Remarkable.

During this, your final year of teaching, rock stars have been idolized, athletes have signed multi-million-dollar contracts before they are old enough to vote, and business leaders have been convicted because of shabby ethics and practices. They have been in the New York Times and you have not. You have stayed in one place, teaching children while controversy swirled over the war in Vietnam, while the Hubble Telescope captured breathtaking pictures of the infant universe, and while the Dow Jones Industrial average went from 750 to 12,000. You have stayed in one place, teaching children, while Elvis died and reappeared in small towns everywhere, while the Berlin Wall fell, and while the nation enjoyed unprecedented prosperity and endured unspeakable terror.

> *A lot happened while you were just sitting around in one place teaching children!*
>
> *There is no profession as important as teaching children and you have done it with rare grace, skill, good humor, and abundant love. You should be the Times Magazine Woman of the Year. You should win multiple Oscars, Tonys, and Emmys. You should be awarded the Pulitzer Prize for Niceness and the Nobel Prize for Dedication. But you won't. Teachers don't become household names unless they do something really awful and all you have done are really wonderful things.*
>
> *Yes, you have taught long enough to visit Pluto and return, yet you have stayed in one place. Some people travel to far galaxies and other people prepare them for the trip. For 35 years you have been Calhoun's NASA. You have inspired and cajoled, taught and hugged. You have given your hundreds of kids a confident and unconditionally affirming start and sewn their flight jackets with threads of wisdom and joy. You've laughed at their 5-year-old jokes and been gob-smacked by their insights. You've wiped their noses (and behinds) and put smiles back on their faces just when they needed it. And because of you, 525 kids believed they could travel to the stars or accomplish anything they wished. And they have. And they will.*
>
> *There can be no life achievement greater than to have affected the lives of 525 humans in a profound and irreversible way. In any other context this statement might be trite, but in your case, it is irrefutably true: You have changed the world for the better.*
>
> Retrieved from http://www.huffingtonpost.com/steve-nelson/teaching-the-most-noble
> -p_b_2471894.html

Happiness and Joy

Happiness is an emotional state often dictated by circumstance. It is not, however, a state of constant euphoria. Instead, happiness is an overall sense of experiencing more positive emotions than negative ones. Being a happy person does not mean you feel happy twenty-four hours per day. That's impossible and completely unnatural. Happy people pursue a career that is fulfilling to them, they make time for their outside interests, and they connect deeply with the people they care about.

Joy is more like a deep, strongly held conviction that is ever-present and unshakeable. *Merriam Webster*'s dictionary defines joy as "the emotion evoked by well-being, success, or good fortune or by the prospect of possessing what one desires." It is a state of mind and an orientation of the heart. It is a settled state of contentment, confidence, and hope. People can have joy while temporarily unhappy. ("I'm upset about the new censures on library books, but I love my role in promoting children's literacy.") And they can have fleeting happiness without joy. ("I'm happy about my pay raise, but I'm wondering if teaching is my true calling.")

When we ask that educators reclaim their joy in education, we are inviting them to revisit their purpose, their self-efficacy, and their passion. We fervently hope educators can renew their sense of satisfaction in their chosen profession as well as revitalize their profound and unflinching faith they are on the right path.

Positivity and Toxic Positivity

People often equate optimism with *positivity*, but there is a difference. Positive thinking does not necessarily mean avoiding or ignoring the bad aspects of life. Instead, it involves making the most of the potentially bad situations, trying to see the best in other people, and viewing ourselves and our abilities in a positive light. Recently, the concept of positivity has come under fire as some educators have rejected what they call *toxic positivity*.

Toxic positivity is the overgeneralization of a happy, optimistic state that results in the denial, minimization, and invalidation of the authentic human emotional experience. Teachers who protest or complain are seen as malcontents and are told simply "to be more awesome." Social media often features unstainable teaching measures—such as individual handshake greetings for every student before every class period and "spontaneous" teacher flash mob dances—as reminders to teachers that they are not doing enough to engage learners. Pinterest and Instagram post photos of picture-perfect classrooms that most teachers know wouldn't last five minutes once real students got in there. (We often caution teachers, "Pinterest is the place you want to visit when you want to feel like a total *loser*!") Joking aside, messages are everywhere telling teachers they are inadequate and are simply not doing enough.

Well-meaning school leaders who constantly push artificial positivity on staff members without allowing for any sort of venting or dissent are often using this facade to avoid talking about the heavy-hitting issues that are important but might make people feel uncomfortable (temporarily, anyway). Teachers get the message that if they are just cheerful enough or work hard enough, everything will work out. Struggling teachers faced with this superficial bromide can be left feeling disconnected, devalued, and desolate.

> In schools, toxic positivity may look like administrators urging teachers to take time for "self-care," but then loading them down with extra meetings and responsibilities. It may look like someone hanging a "teacher strong" banner in the hallway, but not paying for enough soap in the bathroom. It may look like conversations that encourage teachers to

"stay positive," while not digging deeper into the issues that really matter, whether it's a pandemic, equity, or school culture. (Mason, 2021)

Toxic positivity is used to mask deeper, challenging feelings with artificial happiness and contrived merriment. The everything-is-fine mantra can be used to coerce conformity and exert control. Genuine positivity includes compassion, empathy, patience, and grace. It says to coworkers, "We may not be in the same boat, but we are in this storm together."

Positive thinking is about taking a proactive approach to our lives. Instead of feeling hopeless or overwhelmed, positive thinking allows us to tackle life's challenges by looking for effective ways to resolve conflict and come up with creative solutions to problems. Positivity is a prerequisite to both optimism and joy.

Action Step I.2

WHAT IS TOXIC POSITIVITY?

Scan QR Code I.2 to watch the 7-minute TedTalk, *Every Kid Needs a Champion* by Rita Pierson. Some teachers have claimed that administrators who show this video to their staff are promoting toxic positivity. What do you think they are talking about? Do you agree? Why or why not?

How Do We Stay Positive?

In our classrooms, we now have students on medication, students who *need* to be on medication, students who don't speak our language, students who sleep in cars at night, students who don't get to be kids when they go home from school, and students who would rather be anywhere else than at school. We have kids who have lost loved ones because of the pandemic, gun violence, and deportation, and we have kids who endure more heartache in a month than many of us will have to confront in a lifetime. And sometimes, we also teach kids who will never have to work a day in their lives and are already acting like it.

Some educators believe that it is getting harder and harder to make the best of their tough situations. Well-known educator/author Rafe Esquith writes about a teacher he sees frowning one Friday afternoon. When he asks her why she is grumpy on a Friday of all days, she replies, "It just means Monday is that much closer." He concedes that being optimistic is sometimes difficult:

A teacher works hard all day, comes home, and reads an article blaming him or her for the failure of students to do well on tests or behave appropriately. I don't know the exact moment when teachers became the scapegoat for factors beyond their control, but the moment has come. And the unfair, often ridiculous expectations being placed on teachers explain why some of them can't even be happy about an upcoming weekend of family and fun, knowing that Monday looms. (Esquith, 2014, p. 20)

Though we don't dispute Mr. Esquith's point about the pessimistic perceptions and unreasonable expectations teachers often face, we think that too often individuals allow their negative reactions to work circumstances override the otherwise positive aspects of their lives. Teachers have control over more than they realize. After all, we can always determine how we will react to situations. Changing our thought patterns is not easy, but it is a highly effective way to navigate the rough waters of our profession. As Lao Tzu once said, "Thoughts lead to actions, actions lead to habits, habits lead to character, and character changes destiny." So let's talk about changing thoughts.

It's Time to Stop Fretting

In a recent article, *Back to School—Level 8 of Jumanji?* Debbie Silver offers three tips for regaining the joy in teaching in the upcoming school year. She starts by asking educators to stop fretting.

Fretting is a high state of agitation or anxiety over past events or anticipated problems over which one has no control. It can be observed anytime you witness teachers having the "Ain't it awful" conversation. There are legitimate problems in schools right now. Time spent agonizing over events or decisions beyond our control breaks down our resilience and depletes our resourcefulness.

It is possible to acknowledge there are problems while remaining hopeful and confident we can make things better. We can work to fix the fixable and deemphasize the unfixable by coping with it or deemphasizing it. When we intentionally focus our attention and energy on solutions rather than on complaining, we are far more likely to get the results we want or at least make the problems less formidable.

The media would have us believe that our schools are facing insurmountable struggles. We cannot allow ourselves to buy into that line of thought. True, we have lots of work to do, but who can handle it better than this nation's teachers? This year do whatever you need to do to stop fretting—turn off or limit your time with the media, whiners, and colleagues who see themselves as victims. (Silver, 2022)

Let's Take Back Our Power

Teachers need to see ourselves as visionaries, not victims. Most of us have a lot more power than we realize. Think about the students whose lives have been enriched because of you. Consider the times you thought you couldn't cope with some of the challenges in your job, but you did. To maintain our optimism and our self-efficacy, it is essential that we regularly reflect on our areas of achievement and growth.

We need to stretch ourselves and try new things. We should value and acknowledge our valiant efforts. Nothing is more empowering than hard-earned success. We must give ourselves credit for even incremental achievements ("Today, I didn't flip out when that condescending parent asked me if I had even been to college.").

Everyone needs to pay attention to the successes (even the small ones) of those around us. In our community, we can make it a priority to speak well of our school and the people in it. When people ask us what we do, we should proclaim, "I am a teacher!" (or whatever job title you have) with the same gusto Frasier Crane uses when he tells people, "I went to Harvard!" It is an honor to be a part of this profession; let's act like it.

Self-Determination

As experienced teachers, we must admit that each of us has spent some time in the *ain't it awful* place. You know the situation; a bunch of educators gather to collectively bemoan the obstacles that keep us from doing a great job as teachers. It generally starts with someone shaking their head and saying things like, "Well, the principal just informed me that I must cover all my bulletin boards during standardized test week. There's not one thing on those boards that will influence a student's answers, but he says it's a rule that every teacher will cover all informational material on bulletin boards and classroom walls. That is such a waste of time! There is no reason to burden us with such a stupid mandate." The surrounding group members shake their heads in misery as they do the familiar *ain't it awful* routine. No one offers a possible explanation, a plan, or a solution to the challenge. Participants simply hang their heads and say, "Look what **They** are doing to **Us** now. Ain't it Awful?"

Us and **They** are two powerful words that can diminish the optimism within a school. For example, a teacher sends a student to the office and is unhappy about the results. She tells her coworkers, "I sent Draco to the office, and **They** did nothing! I guess the *powers that be* don't care one bit about **Us** and what **We** are having to put up with in our classrooms." Using the term, **They,** in this context is divisive and pits the teachers against those in administration. Laying blame without even trying to find out the facts or seeing the perspective of the other person contributes to an erosion of trust and cooperation among the adults at school. We teachers need to focus more on what we can control rather than trying to micromanage what we perceive others should be doing.

Another problem with the "Look what **They** are doing to **Us**" mentality is that it robs us of power. It suggests that we are helpless against forces that at best do not care about us and at worst are out to get us. Edward Deci and Richard Ryan, University of Rochester, have spent years investigating the general theory of motivation. Their work has influenced over four decades of research on the influence of certain factors supporting the individual's natural or intrinsic tendencies to behave in effective and productive ways. They and others conclude that increasing an individual's autonomy, competency, and relatedness has a positive effect on their *self-determination (SDT)*. And it is self-determination that regulates internalizing and maintaining positive behaviors.

Autonomy

We support the notion that if teachers are connecting with students in a positive way and their students are learning the mandated essential ideas, they (the teachers) should be supported and encouraged to add their own personal styles to the way they teach. This kind of professional freedom is a sure way to boost morale and maintain a more optimistic climate in schools.

We hear from teachers about their increasing feelings of helplessness. Top-down decisions are affecting their freedom to choose the way they teach, the pace at which they teach, and their individuality as educators (some can't even pick their own library books for their rooms).

Along with our current large-scale testing comes large-scale prep and remediation programs (often from the same companies—hmmmm), which prescribe the exact methods and allocated time for instruction. Some of their materials go so far as to script the curriculum to make their lessons *teacher proof*. Perhaps a beginning teacher would welcome a few scripted lessons to practice their new skills for a short while, but for the most part, teachers feel insulted by admonitions to "stick to the script" rather than to creatively address the learning goals with their best practices and based on their knowledge of the students in their classrooms.

After telling teachers for decades to look for teachable moments and to do everything we can to personalize lessons to our students' interests, there is now a push to standardize most every aspect of the classroom experience. Stanford University Education Professor Noddings (2014) writes, "Freedom to plan and teach creatively is conducive to both higher morale and a deeper sense of responsibility" (p. 18).

In her book *Where Teachers Thrive*, Susan M. Johnson pleads for teachers to be given more autonomy and authority in their schools:

> If schools are to become the engine of change that public education needs, then their educators must have sufficient autonomy as a group to make key decisions about staffing, budgeting, curriculum, and the schedule. Whereas school districts have long controlled such matters, school[s] will inevitably be limited in what they can achieve if they are needlessly bound by uniform regulations and expectations. . . . We need a "guided autonomy'" in our schools. (Johnson, 2019, p. 248)

One of the things that attracts educators to the profession is the fundamental understanding that we will be able to make decisions about what goes on in our classrooms. Whether we have long dreamed of replicating our own happy classroom experiences or whether we want to try something entirely different from what we perceived as ineffective when we were in school, we did not aspire to become automatons who merely recite programmed directions and administer summative tests. We believe that teachers should be trusted to communicate essential ideas and to connect with our students in ways we deem most effective. When students are not mastering the knowledge and skills they need or are alienated by a teacher's attitude, corrective action can be taken through peer and/or administrative intervention. Feeling trusted encourages optimism.

There is an old story about a veteran maintenance person who was transferred to a new school. The principal proudly showed him around the campus, instructing him on how he wanted it maintained. In the teacher workroom, the principal made a show of unlocking a large storeroom filled with paper, pencils, and all kinds of supplies and materials a teacher might need to use in her classroom. The principal told the custodian he would be in charge of restocking and maintaining the closet, but that he was to keep it locked at all other times. "We have to keep it secure because we can't trust our teachers with these school supplies."

The old custodian shook his head and asked quietly, "But you trust them with the kids?"

Action Step I.3

TAKE THE HAPPINESS TEST

How do you define optimism? On a scale of 1 to 10 (with 1 being Eeyore and 10 being Pollyanna), where would you put yourself as an optimist?

Scan QR Code I.3 to access the *Psychology Today* Happiness Test. Upon Completion, you will receive a FREE snapshot report with a summary evaluation and graph. You will have the option to purchase the full results, but you don't have to.

Do you agree with the results? Why or why not? (See also Appendix I.2)

●●● DISCUSSION QUESTIONS AND ACTION STEPS

1. How do you feel about Jim Collins's mental image of Admiral Stockdale saying to some of his co-prisoners, "We're not getting out by Christmas; deal with it!" How could that apply to present school challenges?

2. Think back on all the factors that influenced you to become a teacher. Describe both the positive and negative forces that influenced you as you moved toward the job you have now. With your colleagues, try the Appendix I.3 *Life on a Roll* activity.

3. Describe the most optimistic teacher you ever had or presently know. List the qualities about that person that led you to believe they have a positive view of life. What distinguishes that person from other teachers? How did (do) you feel when you were (are) around them?

4. List the factors you think presently deter educators from feeling optimistic. Has your optimism suffered a hit recently? Why or why not?

5. Make a plan to stop *doomscrolling*. Fill your social-media feeds with people and organizations making a positive impact. But be leery of toxic positivity sites that spout platitudes with no substance.

6. Describe the amount of autonomy you feel you have in your classroom. How does that affect how you do your job? What could you do to increase your autonomy?

7. List ten things that cost little or nothing that could be put into place at your school right now that would positively impact teacher morale. Designate two or three group members to share these with your school leaders.

8. Starting now, what are some steps you could take to become a more optimistic educator? What is preventing you from doing that?

9. Make a pact with a colleague or a loved one to text each other at the end of every day with a short list of your best moments in the last twenty-four hours.

Action Steps for School Leaders

1. In the lounge or other central location, put up a Morale Graffiti Board. Encourage staff member to write or draw ideas for improving morale among the adults at school (A suggestion box can work, too.).

2. On a weekly form or in personal conversation, ask some of the following questions of your staff (from *If You Don't Feed the Teachers, They Eat the Students: Guide to Success for Administrators and Teachers* by Connors [2000, p. 22]):

   - How was your week?

   - What are some successes you experienced this week?

   - Did you have any problems this week that the administration team can assist you with?

   - Are than any concerns you have about the overall operation of the school?

   - Do you have any suggestions for improving the school?

   - Do you have any suggestions for the administrative team to improve relationships and strive to achieve our mission?

3. At ball games or at other extracurricular activities, make an announcement asking teachers and staff to stand and be recognized. Let others know about their added efforts to support the students.

(Continued)

(Continued)

4. Write occasional notes to staff members telling them what you value in them and thanking them for how they contribute to the positive morale at your school.

5. Have random drawings throughout the year for staff members that include things like gift cards, weekend get-a-ways, or a half-day sub.

6. If you have young staff members, be mindful of the demands of new parenthood. As much as possible, provide new parents with temporary relief from evening duties, time, a private place for nursing mothers to pump, and occasional late arrival and early departure privileges, if needed. Find someone to fill in for them or volunteer to cover the class yourself.

7. For staff members who are caretakers for aging parents or sick family members, offer occasional late arrival and early departure privileges as well as occasional relief from after school and evening duties. Just knowing that you are aware and supportive goes a long way.

8. Within reason (and always with an eye to safety), let teachers have as much freedom as you can in setting up their classrooms. Painting walls, moving furniture, and decorating to taste gives teachers a sense of autonomy as well as a place to call their own. Their style may not be your style, but uniformity is usually not joyful.

9. Make sure that all staff members have the supplies they need to do their jobs. Stock storerooms (or better yet, individual classrooms) with plenty of tissues, hand sanitizer, paper, cleaning solution, paper towels, band-aids, markers, pens, pencils, and whatever teachers need. Don't make them justify every request.

10. At the beginning of the year, ask every staff member to write down the name of their all-time favorite nonalcoholic drink. At stressful times during the year, surprise them by hand delivering their special beverage. (You don't have to do them all on the same day, but make sure you eventually get around to everyone).

> When given impossible situations with limited resources and time, in every walk of life, educators get the job done. Teachers are the most versatile and heroic workforce on the planet. Every functioning member of society owes a debt to you.
>
> —Williams (as cited in Will, 2022), actor on *Abbot Elementary*

GATHER INFORMATION

In seeking the truth, you have to get both sides of the story.

—Walter Cronkite

Did They Really Put a Litter Box in the Bathroom at School?

In a recent conversation with a friend, we were astonished to hear this young mom lamenting about a newscast she heard that reported a local school district was placing litter boxes in bathrooms for students who identify as cats. This normally well-informed, thoughtful parent said her neighbors and friends on social media were considering pulling their kids out of public schools because, "Schools have gone too far with things like encouraging 'furries.'" We tried to keep a straight face as we offered to do some investigating and get back to her.

Imagine our surprise when we explored this outrageous claim and found it was not isolated to the accused district in Texas. The *New York Times* (Paz, 2022) reports the same allegation was made against Michigan's Midland Public School District. School districts in Iowa, Michigan, and Nebraska have been similarly charged. In none of these areas has the issue of litter boxes been considered or even entertained as a possibility by school boards or administrators.

The news and truth are not the same thing.

—Walter Lippmann

Of course, the erroneous report of kitty litter boxes in bathrooms is just one example of untrue allegations that inundate school and district communities and undermine the constructive work of educators and leaders. It is imperative that both institutions and individuals strive to find truth before making assumptions. That's not easy with the quick availability of misleading data and the timeless power of gossip.

> *Nothing travels faster than the speed of light with the possible exception of bad news, which obeys its own special laws.*
>
> —Douglas Adams

Believing that genuineness is a cornerstone to optimism, we created our first principal for deliberate optimism; 1. Before acting or *reacting*, gather as much information from as many perspectives as possible. In short, gather information. Soon we came up with three more principles. All four principles and an accompanying worksheet can be found in Appendix 1.1 and 1.2.

Principle #1: Gather Information

Perhaps because of the overscheduled, crazy busy lives most of us educators lead, we sometimes rely on others to articulate critical issues impacting our lives. We listen to our preferred news outlet with a naïve belief that it is imparting unbiased facts to us rather than trying to create or spin a story to increase ratings. Instead of reading actual bills or proposals, we receive information about the latest legislative mandate filtered through second-, third-, and fourth-party sources who have their own agendas. And we listen to the one person who actually attended the marathon school board meeting (other than the required participants) and forget that they, too, may be less than objective in the way they saw and report on things that happened.

Someone in the faculty lounge announces, "Well, you are never going to believe what happened at the illustrious school board meeting last night. They are cutting all our health benefits because the superintendent is throwing our district's health insurance to his wife's brother who works for Health-Issues-R-Us!" (Collective gasp.) The informant goes on, "Yes, and that's a fact! My husband and I were there. My Elton had put in a competing bid, which was a far better deal, but they didn't even give his company a chance. As usual, they didn't even try to be fair, and now we're all going to be left with the worst coverage ever. I am so sick and tired of how we are treated in this district. Next thing you know, they'll have the coaches giving us our annual physicals to save on healthcare costs!" Those present are alarmed and begin offering their equally uninformed views and assumptions, painting the worst-case scenarios and generally working themselves into a doom-laden fit about how **They** are always picking on **Us**. What a way to start the day, right?

Or someone returns from a district workshop with the news, "Get ready folks because **They** are completely doing away with cooperative learning!" A lady in my group told me that her cousin's daughter, who is a teacher, said her principal mentioned that he heard it from a reliable source. "**They** are going to prohibit the use of cooperative learning in all core disciplines. It's true! From now on, we won't be allowed to let students work in groups. Can you believe that? Oh my gosh, I don't know what **They** are thinking! I cannot give up my groups. That's the only way I have ever taught. **Those people** are crazy. Most of them haven't been in a classroom in 30 years, and now **They** want to tell **Us** how to teach? I don't think so. That's the last straw for me. I'm going to turn in my resignation, buy a pair of skates, and go be a carhop for Sonic." And the word spreads like head lice. By the end of the day, everyone in your school is preoccupied with the new mandate (which of course, turns out to be completely untrue).

Throughout the book, we talk more about how to avoid this kind of negativism and provide ideas for better choices than just blindly following along or chiming in when problems occur. For now, we want to highlight the point that each of us needs to make every effort to collect accurate information before we react to or act on hearsay.

We're not saying that schools, districts, states, and the federal Department of Education give every issue impartial treatment or that the decisions they make are always fair or even sensible. But we know from experience that it is vital for each of us involved to know as much as possible about impending issues. We need to be aware, realistic, and as informed as possible.

When trying to find authentic answers, we encourage educators to go as directly to the source as possible. If the proper link in the chain of command does not provide precise information, go to the next higher level and keep asking until you get a definitive answer. Consider possible biases and personal agendas of others that sometimes consciously or unconsciously skew information they present. Get as many objective responses as possible, and use your inner compass to navigate a path to the most likely truth.

In the case of the litter box dilemma, one simple phone call to the district's superintendent would have neutralized at least that one false claim. Without any sort of fact-checking, one concerned mom in Michigan made a public proclamation at an open school board meeting that this "nationwide" issue was part of a nefarious issue being pushed upon unwilling communities. She said, "I'm all for creativity and imagination, but when someone lives in a fantasy world and expects other people to go along with it, I have a problem with that" (Paz, 2022). Unfortunately, no one at the meeting responded to her disquieting statements, and a video of her histrionics went viral on social media.

When the matter finally reached the superintendent's attention, he immediately responded with, "It is such a source of disappointment that I felt the necessity to communicate this message to you. . . . Let me be clear in this communication, there is no truth whatsoever to this false statement/accusation! There have never been litter boxes within MPS schools." He went on to urge parents to contact him if rumors like this surfaced again. Problem solved. (We hope.)

The point of discussing the kitty litter box story is to emphasize the need for leaders and educators to be vigilant in not only seeking but also providing accurate information. We wonder why the officials in the MPS boardroom did not pause the parent's address to ask for a fact check. Too many times, our silence is perceived as agreement. In our current contentious, divisive atmosphere we must speak up with honesty and with facts.

Action Step 1.1

FACT CHECK

Scan QR Code 1.1 to watch this MediaWise video featuring a teen fact checker who investigates the litter box controversy. Think about how your school or district could do something like this to help diffuse erroneous rumors, gossip, and assumptions.

With intentionality, we need to help quiet the hyperactive beehive mindset surrounding our schools. School administrator, Gaskell (2022), talks about his already pandemic-stressed school community being overwhelmed by a "toxic groupthink" stemming from news about increasing school tragedies. His answer is to try to override parents' emotionally charged spontaneous reactions with logic and practical thinking, "Students have a far lower chance of being harmed in school than almost any other risk they face including traveling to and from school, catching a potentially deadly disease, and suffering from a life-threatening injury through interscholastic sports."

Gaskell believes in a proactive approach that teaches both parents and students how to get better at filtering information they find online. He recommends assisting students and families in managing constant distractions from alarming new cycles. He regularly discusses with students and parents valid methods by which they can guard against getting caught up in media frenzy and become discerning evaluators of information from every source.

We think it is additionally beneficial to be candid about the harm caused to all by unconfirmed accusations, idol gossip, and self-serving agitation. Schools should shine a spotlight on misinformation and provide a space where parents, teachers, students, leaders, and other community members can find up-to-date factual information.

Fear of the unknown, constant threat warnings, and negative "hives" promote pessimism, loss of self-efficacy, and hopelessness in each of us. Having trustworthy sources for data contributes to overall realistic optimism. Educators and leaders need to both seek clarity for themselves and take an active role in providing the tools others need to make informed decisions. Our goal is to pursue a realistic awareness toward what is happening around us.

Guiding Questions on Realistic Awareness

Before we buy into or begin reacting to what is being disseminated as *the truth*, it is our responsibility to ask ourselves some guiding questions:

1. Who exactly is "**They**?" Are we talking about a person, a committee, a voting body, or some other entity? It's important to know exactly who is responsible for the alleged decision.

2. Have I done my own research/fact checking on the current education issue or topic?

3. Have I sought out and listened to at least two sides of the issue or topic?

4. Have I relied on the words of others to help form my opinion? If so, have I considered their possible biases and credibility?

5. Have I tried to separate the facts from my preconceptions about those who made the decision (including attributing motives based on my assumptions)?

6. Was there an opportunity for me or for other affected parties to voice our opinions about the matter before a decision was made?

(Continued)

(Continued)

7. Are we as a staff waiting to react or are we looking to begin a proactive approach to the problem?

8. Have we looked closely at the data used to support the new mandate?

9. Have we made an effort to contact similar schools or districts that have already implemented this program?

10. Have we as a staff dissected the full potential impact (pros and cons) on ourselves, our school, our community, and most importantly, our students?

Reviewing and reflecting on these questions might take time, but in the long run, the process will encourage helpful deliberations and perhaps influence those around us to think carefully before drawing conclusions. A worksheet for this purpose is provided in Appendix 1.3.

Filtering Our Perception of Others' Motives

Principle #1 suggests that before making a judgment about anything, we gather as much information from as many varied sources as possible. Sometimes our view of human behavior is erroneously flawed by the way we interpret the motives of others. It is never a good idea to assume that we know explicitly why another person acts as they do. The way humans accommodate and assimilate the world around them is highly influenced by their personal learning and thinking style. We need to consider our own tendencies as well as develop an awareness for those who respond to their environment in ways that can be totally different from ours.

Action Step 1.2

WHAT IS YOUR MIND STYLE?

Before you begin the next section, it would be helpful to take the Mind Styles Test. Scan QR Code 1.2.

Education is a people business. Daily, we interact not only with our students but also with colleagues, administrators, support staff, parents, and a myriad of adults who are invested in the business of school. To maintain our optimism, we must figure out a way to consider the daunting opinions and behaviors of others through an objective lens. Gathering information entails taking the time to understand the positions and approaches of others. A good place to start is to understand the learning styles of those with whom we need to connect.

In our experience, we have found that seemingly off-putting behavior is sometimes most notable when groups are trying to implement change. Unfortunately, some people adhere to the *I don't mind change as long as I don't have to do anything differently* credo. But is that really what they truly mean? If we look a little deeper, could it be that they are basically trying to accommodate new policies and new procedures in a way that best suits their inherent styles? Perhaps they are not trying so much to "rain on our parades" as to deal with challenges in the best way they know how.

Gregorc's Four Mind Styles
··

Dr. Gregorc (1984), author of the *Mind Styles Model*, is a phenomenological researcher and author who studies the different ways people best acquire and assimilate new information. His belief is that people inherently differ in the manner they approach problem solving and the ways they make sense of their environments. He writes, "It appears that dispositions for interacting with the world in specific ways are inborn." His longstanding investigation into thinking styles has led to some interesting thoughts. Perhaps the behavior that outsiders perceive as antisocial, fussy, compulsive, flighty, frivolous, and the like are just compensatory ways that certain people make sense of their worlds. Maybe if we better understood the needs of people with different thinking styles, we could start to see that they are not trying to go against us or to be difficult but rather they are doing what comes naturally to them when coping with life.

Dr. Gregorc believes the mind works on a **perceptual** level and on an **ordering** level. Perceptual qualities generally lean toward concrete or abstract.

> *Concrete:* This quality enables you to register information directly through your five senses: sight, smell, touch, taste, and hearing. When you are using your concrete ability, you are dealing with the obvious, the "here and now." You are not looking for hidden meanings or making relationships between ideas or concepts. "It is what it is."

> *Abstract:* This quality allows you to visualize, to conceive ideas, to understand or believe that which you

cannot see. When you are using your abstract quality, you are using your intuition, your imagination, and you are looking beyond "what is" to the more subtle implications. "It is not always what it seems."

Gregorc thinks that an individual's ordering ability normally manifests itself as sequential or random.

Sequential: Allows your mind to organize information in a **linear**, step-by-step manner. When using your sequential ability, you are following a logical train of thought, a traditional approach to dealing with information. You may also prefer to have a plan and to follow it rather than rely on impulse.

Random: Lets your mind organize information by **chunks** and in no particular order. When you are using your random ability, you may often be able to skip steps in a procedure and still produce the desired result. You may even start in the middle or at the end and work backwards. You may also prefer your life to be more impulsive or spur of the moment than planned. (Gregorc, n.d.)

Dr. Gregorc (1982) believes that even though both ordering abilities are present in individuals, people are generally more comfortable using one than the other. His classifications are determined by the strongest perceptive abilities paired with the compelling ordering abilities, and they are as follows:

1. Concrete sequential (CS)

2. Abstract random (AR)

3. Abstract sequential (AS)

4. Concrete random (CR)

No one style is better or more advantageous than the others; each of the four is simply a different way of dealing with life. While no one is totally one style, most people default to one of these categories because of their basic inclinations. Following are descriptions of people in each of the groups. See if you can find yourself, as well as identify some behaviors in others that are typical for their learning styles.

CONCRETE SEQUENTIAL

The concrete sequential is a lover of neatness, order, and detail. They want specific directions and do not like to be distracted when learning. Their preference is to do one activity at a time. They like direct instruction with hands-on practice. Their approach to change is slow and incremental. They like to be in control of most situations, and they do not like surprises. They avoid unpredictable people and circumstances. They like to work in quiet, controlled environments.

The concrete sequential is factual, organized, dependable, and punctual. Most CSs believe that you are, in fact, a little late if you show up right on time. They are hardworking, consistent, and accurate. They are great at following directions and meeting deadlines. They are usually conservative and always consistent.

Does this sound like you or someone you know? Depending on your own style, you may or may not be able to relate to this person because they have a hard time working in groups. It's difficult for them to delegate tasks because others "won't do it right." Dealing with abstract ideas or requests to "use your imagination" is also not easy for them. They are uncomfortable in unorganized environments, and they prefer to make changes in a limited, methodical, supported manner.

If this is not your style, you may see them as a bit fussy with a tendency toward being a control freak. You may resent them for wanting to do things in a particular order and insisting that the rest of you follow all the rules. You may feel like they don't ever want to change so you give up on them. However, what if you reframed your thinking by changing your beliefs about this person? Instead of labeling them a nitpicking perfectionist out to ruin every new idea, what if you acknowledge they really need to have a logically sequenced, well-structured challenge to feel comfortable?

Perhaps it would be helpful to take the extra effort to make sure when you present your ideas to this colleague that you focus on step-by-step instructions and real-life examples. Taking the time to see the valuable organizational skills this person has to offer will help you not only view them in a more favorable light but will also help them feel more valued and probably more cooperative. Often this person is a great choice for a team leader.

ABSTRACT RANDOM

Is there someone with whom you work that wakes up in a new world every day? Does this person constantly lose their train of thought, switch subjects with no warning, and bounce around like Tigger in *Winnie the Pooh*? It sounds as though we are describing someone with ADHD, but in reality, there is a learning style called *abstract random*, which manifests characteristics very similar to some of those identified with the ADHD Syndrome.

Abstract randoms are spontaneous, flexible, and quick to "jump on the bandwagon" if they believe in the idea. This individual is sensitive, compassionate, perceptive, and sentimental. They pay attention to human detail. This is the colleague who notices if you've lost weight, if you've done something different with your hair, or if you are worried about something outside of school. They are usually people pleasers who love to bring together all sorts of folks for discussions, activities, or just hanging out. They are lively, colorful, and full of energy and are comfortable in busy environments.

On the other hand, the abstract random has a great deal of trouble dealing with people who are bossy, negative, or unfriendly. They prefer to multitask rather than work on one thing at a time. They have difficulty following rules and restrictions, and they have trouble accepting even positive criticism.

ARs are generally poor time managers, and they sometimes fail to finish projects they start. People not of this ilk sometimes see them as flaky, outlandish, or just plain weird. They doubt the AR's substance and don't trust them with anything important. ARs prefer to jump right in and deal with the consequences later. In meetings, they enjoy talking off topic and dealing with feelings rather than facts.

If you are not an AR, you may be reticent to deal with one. However, if you look at this person under a different lens, maybe you can see that they do have substance but they sometimes don't show it because they're always off on the next tangent when you are still finalizing the steps in the previous one (which, by the way, is one they started and lost interest in). With the understanding that ARs are extremely sensitive and in tune with others, maybe you could simply say to them, "Sue, can you slow down a bit? I love that you always have new ideas, but we really need you to help finish this project first. You are quite the cheerleader, and we really could use your enthusiasm to complete this part before we go on."

Rather than dismiss the AR as someone you can't count on, it's probably more productive to focus on their ability to listen to others and to energize others' efforts. You eventually might be able to help them recognize how strongly their emotions affect their concentration.

ABSTRACT SEQUENTIAL

You would think that with four thinking styles, you could expect to find about 25 percent of educators in each category. You would be wrong. It has been our experience that generally less than 10 percent of faculties and staff are abstract sequentials. ASs are found in abundance at the university level, but not so much in K–12 settings. The reason there are few of them in traditional schools is evident when you examine who they are. ASs thrive on research and do not like being hurried to make a decision. They like to have the time to thoroughly explore a topic before moving on. They prefer to direct their own learning and to work alone. They are highly skeptical and dislike distractions.

The abstract sequential at your school may be a person who demands references for everything you state. They want to know the credentials of the person or persons behind the idea you are proposing, and they have little patience with small talk or sentimental rhetoric. It's not that they are unwilling to change, but you are never going to win them over with a moving story, well-timed music, or a group hug. They need to see facts and figures. They are voracious readers, but they often fail to pick up on social cues. (Think of Sheldon Cooper on the *Big Bang Theory*).

ASs have great difficulty working with people who have differing opinions from theirs. If left unchecked, they can monopolize the conversation with little awareness of the feelings of others. Their motto is "knowledge is power." Behind their backs, you may call them "Ms. or Mr. Know-It-All" or something less kind. You may feel that they don't value you or your feelings so you avoid them when you can.

The problem with dismissing the abstract sequential is that you are missing an opportunity to relate to someone who is excellent at applying logic or finding solutions to problems. Due to their extensive reading, they probably have a wealth of knowledge they could share with you and your colleagues. Their analysis of the finer points of issues and proposals can provide invaluable information when trying to reach a decision. This is the person who not only enjoys doing the research but also is able to tease out the key points and significant details.

So rather than feeling defensive and oppressed by this person, why not consider that hurting your feelings is not their intent? Like all of us, they have their own peculiarities that are born from their need to deal with the world in a way that makes them comfortable. When they correct you or question you about your thinking, just understand that they probably don't mean it as an attack. They really want to know how you came to your conclusion. Be aware that they are more persuaded by facts than by emotion and they have little regard for hearsay.

CONCRETE RANDOM

The concrete random often has the philosophy, "If it ain't broke, break it!" Like concrete sequentials, they are based in reality, but because of their random nature, they generally like change just because they are ready for something different. Sometimes they are the instigators of change. This person is inquisitive and independent. They do not read directions, but instead, they solve everything with a trial-and-error approach. They get the gist of ideas quickly and demonstrate the uncanny ability to make intuitive leaps when exploring unstructured problem-solving experiences. They are usually self-motivated and not interested in details.

The CRs on your staff are often a technology specialists, science teachers, or people involved in an innovative disciplines. They have an experimental attitude about everything, and they sometimes go off on their own leaving their colleagues behind. CRs have a strong need to do things in their own way. They do not like formal reports, keeping detailed records, routines, or redoing anything once it is done. Sometimes CRs are seen as mavericks who are too independent and poor team players, but that isn't necessarily true.

CRs have a tremendous capacity for accepting many different kinds of people as well as offering unique ways of doing things. They contribute unusual and creative ideas, and they are able to visualize the future. Rather than trying to rein them in, you can support their investigational approach to life and get them to help you explore your own preconceived barriers.

Because they are usually risk takers, CRs can benefit from working with sequentials—who are usually more able to anticipate possible pitfalls and trouble spots as well as adhere to deadlines. Sometimes others are put off by a perceived impatience in a CR, but upon closer examination, you may find that they are just colleagues who want to be doing rather than talking. These adventurous individuals can spark creativity in others with their intuitive, innovative thinking. As with the other three learning styles, CRs have their challenges as well as their positive qualities.

One major step toward accepting others is realizing that every style has its tradeoffs. Strength in one area is often counterbalanced by a weakness in another. Taking the time and patience to understand the true nature of a colleague's idiosyncrasies can lead to a huge payoff in building a connection with that person. Changing your beliefs about why they make some of the choices they do can change the manner in which you view and react to them. Reclaiming your joy for teaching starts with rebuilding your relationships with those who share the work you do.

THE GREGORC STYLE DELINEATOR

We recommend that the adults at school take the Gregorc Style Delineator (or some other instrument that explores basic life approaches) together and discuss the implications of their results. Generally, individuals are delighted to be able to put a finger on why some people act the way they do. We find it rewarding when interacting adults start to realize that many things that get on their last nerve (with both adults and students) are just coping mechanisms of the offending party intrinsic to their mind style. It is much easier to tolerate the habitual lateness of a colleague when we realize they are one of the randoms and probably have no idea what time it is rather than attributing it to some kind of passive-aggressive act directed toward us. Just changing the labels from "He's so anal retentive," to "Well, that's his concrete sequential nature," is a positive step toward building community. The Gregorc Style Delineator is available for purchase online.

Gregorc's Mind Styles Model can certainly provide insight into human behavior. His theory is not the only one out there, nor is it universally accepted. However, learning and thinking about different ways that people process information undoubtedly helps us be more empathetic communicators. We can't control how other people internalize things we say and do, but we can control our intentions and how we respond when we unintentionally hurt or alienate others. Whatever thinking style, learning preference, multiple intelligence, or personality theory you subscribe to, we think it's important to gather information and think deeply about the way humans act and interact. After all, dealing with humans (both big and little) is our primary job.

We address other aspects of gathering information about human behavior in Chapter 6, but for now, consider what kinds of evidence to you need to collect to remain positive in your attitude and in your relationships with others.

●●● DISCUSSION QUESTIONS AND ACTION STEPS

1. Where do you get the majority of your information about school? What about information on the world in general? Do you think your source(s) influences the way you feel about things? Do you think other people's source(s) of information influences their attitudes about things? If so, in what ways?

2. Consider the story floating around the internet about the litter box in the students' restrooms or name some other egregious report that has been recounted in your district. Discuss how and why such narratives gain so much traction. What can you as an individual or as a team do when confronted with false or misleading information?

(Continued)

(Continued)

3. Pick a current hot issue at school. Use the steps in Appendix 1.3 *Realistic Awareness* to further explore the topic. Did using the steps expand your ideas about the subject? Why or why not?

4. Where do you direct students and parents to go when seeking accurate information about your classroom, school, or district? Why?

5. Is there a negative "hive" affecting your school community? Identify it (them) and list positive actions you have done or could do to help counteract their influence.

6. Think of an instance where you misjudged a person's intent or motive. Why do you think you made an incorrect assumption? How can you avoid making inaccurate conjectures about why others make the choices they do?

7. After taking the Mind Styles Test [see QR Code 1.2] and reading the descriptions of the four mind styles in this chapter, do you agree with how you scored? Why or why not?

8. How can considering information about areas such as mind styles improve our interactions with others?

9. How would our human relations be improved if each of us began every interaction with the assumption that others were operating with good intentions?

10. In a meeting of more than 10 people, play the children's game, Gossip (search online for Gossip Game Ideas [Benac, 2017]). Discuss how rumors and gossip interfere with the idea behind Principle #1: Gather Information.

Action Steps for School Leaders

1. Plan a staff meeting to introduce or reinforce the Four Principles of Deliberate Optimism. Lead a group in using the four principles to deal with a present school-wide issue.

2. Acquaint parents and the community with the Four Principles of Deliberate Optimism by adding the principles to school newsletters and other school publications as well as discussing them in PTO, PTA, or similar meetings.

3. Have the Four Principles of Deliberate Optimism printed for every staff member. You can use laminated pocket cards, squeeze balls, posters, or whatever suits the style of your school community.

4. Establish a place (newsletter, website, social media site, etc.) for parents, teachers, community members, and students to go to for straight facts and information. Keep it up to date; make it as transparent as possible.

5. In the most diplomatic manner possible, shine a spotlight on agitators, gossip mongers, and misinformation specialists. Provide accurate, updated information and politely ask them to avoid inflammatory rhetoric and get their facts straight before posting information.

6. When there is a problem (e.g., teachers arriving late for duty assignments), speak directly to those responsible. Blanket emails or general announcements at faculty meetings are usually ignored by the transgressors and are demoralizing to those who are doing what they are supposed to do.

7. Post a "Chain of Command" type flowchart for both parents and teachers to see. Let them know the most effective course to take for getting their needs met (e.g., calling the superintendent at home to complain about Vincent's drop from an A- to a B- in art class is not the best place to start).

8. Periodically administer inventories, questionnaires, and fun quizzes to teachers and staff to gather more information about them as individuals. With their permission, post their birthdays, special events, interests, talents, accreditations, learning goals, and so forth, so that you and others can gather insights about who they are.

9. If you don't already have one, establish a hospitality committee that will oversee team-building events and fun activities appropriate for the staff members at your school.

10. Using an asset-based approach, look at unique gifts and preferred ways of learning among staff members. Shape professional development and other activities around their strengths with personalized learning experiences. For additional suggestions, see Appendix 1.4 *Recognizing and Celebrating Staff*.

11. Set up a suggestion box so that questions and ideas can be posted anonymously. Address as many as you can and try to acknowledge the ones you cannot do (e.g., At a faculty meeting, you might state, "I'd like to acknowledge the request I got from one of you to limit the number of students in each of your sections to twenty-four. Unfortunately, with our present number of students and teachers, that is not possible, but I'm willing to look at a more equitable way to balance classes if you'll write me or come by my office and give me more details about your particular situation." Or, "I'd like to acknowledge the request for me to take a long walk off a short pier, but I really need you to be a bit more specific about what is bothering you.").

CONTROL WHAT YOU CAN

Everything can be taken from a man but one thing: the last of the human freedoms—to choose one's attitude in any given set of circumstances, to choose one's own way.

—Frankl (1946) *Man's Search for Meaning*

We cannot control the fact that there's suffering in the world, but we can control whether we contribute to it or help alleviate it. Henderson (2013) correctly maintains, "Educators cannot eradicate poverty, remove neighborhood gangs, stop cultural violence, heal parental addictions, or prevent the myriad of other types of stress, risk, and trauma many students face daily." Likewise, we cannot as individuals stop widespread abuse, neglect, lack of parental support, debilitating health and learning disorders, or any manner of large-scale cases of social injustice.

We cannot control which students come to our schools and which ones leave. We do not get to decide how school or district resources are allocated. We don't even have the final say in what grade, discipline, or even what curriculum we teach. But there are some things we can control—that's what this chapter is about.

What You Can't Control

JOB PLACEMENT

Of course, part of our job placement is determined by our degree(s) earned, our area(s) of certification, and perhaps even our experience in a particular field. Schools are required to provide documentation to the state that we are qualified for the job assignment we have. In emergencies, such as the present teaching shortage, a teacher can teach out of field, but for the most part, certain certifications are required to teach in specific areas. We usually warn teacher candidates to be careful about the certifications they earn. If you have a certification to teach high school humanities and somewhere along the way you also acquired a certification in PreK–K instruction, your district can compel you to teach a kindergarten class (even if you'd rather have a root canal sans painkillers than teach those little *hyperactive petri dishes*). Even tenure normally only stipulates that you will have a job but not which job you will have. In some districts, teacher unions have negotiated a bit more individual power in job selection, but for the most part, when you are hired by a district, you have no legal right to say which school you prefer or what you will teach.

CURRICULUM

Today in some communities, there are heated discussions going on about what is taught in local classrooms. Sometimes, individual teachers are misinformed about who has the right to dictate curriculum. While teachers generally have the right to decide how they choose to present their subject matter, it is the constitutional right of the states to decide what they want to be taught in their schools. Sometimes, states allow individual districts to make decisions within the state framework, but it is basically the state's responsibility to oversee curriculum.

It is not a teacher's right to decide what curriculum they are going to teach in their classrooms. Standards and essential ideas are determined outside the individual teacher's responsibility level. Consequently, time spent wailing over curriculum choices to people who are not decision makers is wasted. There are appropriate long-term solutions in which a teacher can become involved (writing letters, volunteering to serve on committees, talking to decision makers), but for the most part, like job placement, the decisions are not ours to make. (See Chapter 4 for more ideas about how to become an educational proponent.)

It is our contention that while we support the states' right to determine curriculum and establish standards, we wholeheartedly support the individual teacher's right to determine how and when we teach the mandated curriculum. The point is that constantly wringing our hands over things we cannot change is a waste of time and one sure way to lose our optimism. There are many things we can control, and those are the areas in which we need to focus our positive energy and our resources. One of the most important factors in reclaiming our optimism is to acknowledge those things we cannot control and work around them.

WHAT YOU CAN'T CONTROL	WHAT YOU CAN CONTROL
Curriculum—usually decided by the state or local district	How you use the curriculum to engage students and lead them to success.
Job placement—guidelines provided by the local district	Learning everything you can about your assigned grade-level and subject matter to assure students achieve.
Colleagues' attitudes—some are worn down, worn out, or just not meant to be in teaching	Keep yourself healthy and upbeat. Use encouragement instead of argument.
Student context—everything from neglected to over-protection	Make every day in your class a lesson in stability and thoughtful decision-making.
Parent expectations—the best for their child but sometimes unreasonable	Communicate with parents in every way possible. Build relationships.

"Well, Okay Then . . ."
The Story of Mrs. Touhy

There are people who are able to put things into perspective and continue toward their goals no matter what the obstacles. The movie, *The Blindside*, portrays the story of Michael Oher, a famous football player who played for three NFL teams, including the 2013 Super Bowl-winning Baltimore Ravens. The movie chronicles his life as a young African American raised in poverty and neglect who eventually is embraced, then adopted by a conservative Caucasian family in Tennessee—the Touhys.

Predictable obstacles occur throughout the story, but one of the things that inspires us is the way Michael's new guardian, Leigh Anne Touhy, meets each one. She listens closely, considers the problem, and gives the same answer each time, "Well, okay then." In other words, she tells Michael that she understands the obstacles, she hears what he is saying, and now she's ready to regroup and try another route.

"Well, Okay Then . . ." for Educators

It seems to us that a majority of teachers have long embraced Leigh Anne Touhy's, "Well, okay then" philosophy. Despite budget cuts, incomprehensible mandates, solutions-du-jour program adoptions, students who arrive at school ill-prepared and sometimes ill-cared for, virtual and hybrid teaching, and countless other challenges we face daily, most teachers have always been able to evaluate the situation, consider all the factors, and start over with the attitude of Mrs. Touhy, "Well, okay then." It's not fun, and it's not happy. Perhaps the only way to sustain this kind of hopeful, down-to-business nature is to believe in the power of our influence, to trust in a larger purpose, and to have clearly defined long-term goals. Teachers must believe that what we do matters and what we accomplish has meaning beyond short-term data aggregation and subjective judgments from those who have little or no idea about the components of effective education.

What we are talking about is not a goal of continual thrill but rather an overarching hopefulness and confidence about the future successful outcomes of our efforts. The optimism we support is not some vague hope that eventually things will all work out but rather a positive, realistic conviction that we have control over certain aspects of our jobs and no control over others. Most of us have a lot more power than we realize, and all of us can choose how we react to those things we cannot control. We can throw up our hands and say, "I can't do this," or we can look a challenge in the eye and say, "Well, okay then, I'll try it another way."

Find Ways to Circumvent Barriers

An elementary science teacher is assigned to teach hands-on science to third- through fifth-grade students. Her room is a temporary building standing alone in the middle of the playground. She has no reasonable access to running water. She tells her administrator that she needs available water to provide students with the hands-on experiences she wants them to have. She is told there is no budget for plumbing her room for water, so she will just have to work around the problem. "Well, okay then."

Action Step 2.2

BRAINSTORMING INNOVATIVE PRACTICAL SOLUTIONS

Imagine you are this teacher—what could you do? Think of as many practical solutions as you can. Be innovative. If you are in a book study group, stop here and brainstorm ideas before reading further. If you are reading this by yourself, stop just a minute and try to think of ideas before reading on. Seriously, stop reading until you have thought of at least three ideas.

BUT WHAT IF . . .

An ingenious teacher we know arranged with the school custodian to run a water hose with an attached spray nozzle from the closest outdoor spigot through one of her classroom windows and into a bucket in her classroom. On days she needed water, she turned on the outdoor faucet and left the nozzle closed until she needed water. She got a local store to donate large plastic tubs for basins, and all she had to do was squeeze the handle on the nozzle when she wanted to run water. Afterward, the students poured the non-contaminated water onto grass around the building. Both she and the students enjoyed having the water they needed to do the wonderfully messy activities she planned.

It would be easy to start picking this one solution apart. Sometimes negative people's knee-jerk response to a creative solution is, "But what if . . . ?" Teachers in colder climates may ask what happens when it's freezing outside? Those located on the second floor of a building might dismiss the idea as too impractical for them.

PE teachers might object to having a garden hose running across a playing field. Maybe the windows at your school don't open. All of those are valid objections, but forward-thinking teachers focus less on what won't work and spend more time on what will. When we are hamstrung with the idea of how awful it is for a teacher to be put in that situation in the first place, we stop seeking solutions. Teachers are the most creative, innovative, resourceful people we know (mainly because we *have* to be), and we believe our challenge as realistic optimists is to find what works in our particular situations. Once we have the most clear, realistic view of perceived obstacles, we need to give ourselves permission to move on from things beyond our control (and there are many of those).

SPORADIC, CATASTROPHIC CIRCUMSTANCES

One beautiful Friday in August 2005, I (Debbie) worked in a school located in Harvey, a suburb of New Orleans. I led the teachers through a series of activities designed to foster a positive school environment. At lunch, the teachers and I made plans for how the staff could start turning the school around beginning the following Monday. I then caught a flight to the west coast to make another presentation. While leading a workshop for teachers in California on that Monday, I was informed that Hurricane Katrina had hit the coast of Louisiana and the levees had been breached. The school I had been in the Friday before was completely gutted. Teachers and students in Harvey lost homes, neighborhoods, and the complete infrastructure of their schools. I wept with shock and frustration when I learned of the horrific loss of lives and property, and I considered the irony of the timing on their well-intentioned school improvement plans.

In 2013, seven students at Plaza Towers Elementary were killed when a tornado ravaged their school in Moore, Oklahoma. Educators and community members were devastated by the incomprehensible loss of so much in such a short period of time. Schools in the United States and abroad are affected by overwhelming natural disasters, which though infrequent, are mind-numbing in their impact.

More frequent are the premature deaths of students, faculty, and school family members caused by disease, auto accidents, and freakish twists of fate. And of course, a growing problem is deaths by murder, gang wars, terrorists, and emotionally unbalanced students, which have wreaked havoc on school campuses across our nation and beyond. The impact of these outside negative forces can be felt at every level of newly implemented school safety policies and procedures. Because of the horror of the recent escalation in school shootings, some feel that their buildings are no longer safe places.

In March of 2020, our nation and much of the world responded to the COVID-19 pandemic with a shelter-in-place mandate. Teachers were tasked with shifting to new platforms for reaching and teaching students in turn-around periods between twenty-four hours to just over one week. Most were given very little direction or support as they struggled to learn new technology and shift instruction and assessment to online. The whole situation was unprecedented, unchartered, and more than a bit chaotic. Some teachers were unable to reach all their students and were left with a fear of what was happening to their "ghost pupils."

While stories of such heartbreaking disasters try our souls, we know that teachers are usually among the first ones on the scene to help restore order and assist in instilling a sense of security for kids. We change course instantaneously to adapt to the needs of our students. There are indeed circumstances where life just gets in the way of even our best plans. And after the initial shock wears off, we say, "Well, okay then." We know we must pick up the pieces and move forward with what we are able to control.

Positive Reframing

It is true that we cannot change some of our least favorite things about our circumstances, but we can always change the way we deal with our situations. We can't always control our thoughts and feelings, but we can control whether we attach to them, identify with them, or act on them. A powerful tool for dealing with the challenging times educators now face is called *positive reframing*.

Action Step 2.3

POSITIVE REFRAMING

Scan QR Code 2.3 to watch a 5-minute video on positive reframing. Think about something presently troubling you that might not be so disconcerting if you thought about it differently. Jot down some ways you might reframe the issue in a more positive light.

Positive reframing gives our minds a break from being worn down by negative events and thoughts. It involves thinking about a negative or challenging situation in a more positive way. This could involve thinking about a benefit or upside to a negative situation that you had not considered. Alternatively, it can involve identifying a lesson to be learned from a difficult situation.

Another form of positive reframing is finding something to be grateful for in a challenging situation. For example, your administrator, a much-loved member of your school, has been transferred to a struggling school across town. Rather than focusing on how much you will miss her and your fear of who her replacement will be, you could be grateful for the time you had with her and think about the systems she put in place at your school that will continue without her presence. You can look forward to working with a leader who may have innovative ideas and a fresh approach. You can be hopeful that the other school will benefit from your mentor's leadership as did your campus. You have no control over your administrator's transfer, but you do have control over how you react to it.

The way you frame (look at) an event or situation will influence the way you feel about it. Negative thinking patterns affect our feelings, our reactions, our decision making, and ultimately our lives. It is not easy, but it is essential for optimism that we learn to control the way we view things.

Action Step 2.4

REFRAMING UNHELPFUL THOUGHTS

Scan QR Code 2.4 to watch a 1.5-minute video, *Reframe Unhelpful Thoughts*. The video gives a quick, concise overview of changing negative thought patterns.

Seligman and Deliberate Optimism

Most of us are familiar with the term "learned helplessness." It is a sociological expression generally used in education to refer to students who are not only reluctant learners but who believe there is no way they can improve their circumstances. They think bad things happen to them through misfortune and not because of logical consequences of their choices. Unfortunately, those students often grow up to be helpless, hopeless, bitter adults who are caught in a cycle of failure because their beliefs create actions that create circumstances that reinforce their original beliefs. In every sense, they have learned to be helpless.

In studying learned helplessness, Dr. Seligman and Maier (1967) conditioned a group of dogs by punishing them with electrical shocks. The dogs learned they had no control over when the shocks started or stopped. Later, the researchers put the conditioned dogs in a double-sided shuttle box that had a shocking side and a non-shocking side. A low-retaining barrier separated the two chambers. Though placed on the shock side, dogs were free to step over the low barrier to the non-shock side. However, the dogs did not attempt to step over the barrier to the shock-free zone. They simply lay down on top of the shocking coils and howled. They were inches away from relief, but they made no attempt to help themselves. From his observations Seligman derived the term, "learned optimism."

Later, Dr. Seligman decided to try to teach learned helplessness to humans. Thankfully, he did not use a shocking mechanism on people. Instead, he used loud sound to provide an irritant to members of the control group. He was surprised to find that unlike with dogs, he could not always condition people to be helpless. Many subjects refused to feel powerless. Even though he attempted to condition them to believe they could not control the loud noise, several subjects refused to stop trying. They seemed to draw from an inner strength and would not accept that they were doomed to accepting the loud noise. Since those early experiments, he has continued to study and write about what factors are important for building resiliency and tenacity in people. When he was president of the American Psychiatric Association, he challenged his colleagues to quit focusing on why people have psychological problems and start working on how to help them live better lives. He believes that humans can learn to be optimistic by *unlearning* nonproductive thought patterns.

Nonproductive Thought Patterns Include

- Taking everything personally

- Downplaying positive events

- Feeling like a victim who is helpless

- Expecting the worst

- Focusing on the negatives

- All or nothing thinking

- Believing that feelings are facts

- Drawing big conclusions with little or no evidence

Seligman originated a plan he calls the "ABC Method." He believes that if you want to lead an optimistic life, you must learn to argue with yourself in a non-negative way. In his book, *Learned Optimism: How to Change Your Mind and Your Life* (Seligman, 2006), he describes how we can learn to lead ourselves into hope and action instead of despair.

The ABC Model

Adversity: The bad event or challenge you face.

Belief: Your default thinking or belief about the bad event or challenge. It's your explanation and interpretation of why things have gone wrong.

Consequences: The impact of your beliefs. It's what you feel and what you do because of your belief or interpretation of what happened.

Our four principles of deliberate optimism parallel Seligman's ABC Model in that both ask participants to describe accurately the source of their angst, to examine more than one assumed motive for the cause, and to consider the long-term effect of our selected actions.

As an example, let's say your principal just informed you that next year instead of teaching the sixth-grade physical science classes you have taught for the past seven years, he is reassigning you to teach eighth-grade earth science classes. You are appalled. You already have done years of work gathering resources and preparing the lessons you use in teaching physical science. You assume you are being punished for some transgression, and you cannot believe you will no longer be teaching your favorite age group and preferred content. You just know that you will be stuck teaching eighth grade from now on, and you don't even like earth science. You are inconsolable about this change in your career; everyone knows how much you love teaching sixth grade, so this must be some kind of personal vendetta. Let's apply the ABC Method to this scenario.

Adversity: You are being switched from teaching sixth-grade physical science to eighth-grade earth science.

Belief: You believe this decision was made to punish you in some way and that you will be stuck with teaching your least favorite science for the rest of your time at that school. Teaching earth science will never be as much fun as teaching physical science.

Consequences: You are hurt, angry, and fearful. You would like to get even with whoever made this decision. You know you are going to hate teaching earth science and you are not too crazy about teaching eighth graders. You decide you will let everyone know how unhappy you are and will stop doing all the many extras you do to help around the school.

It is easy to get caught up in our protected *teaching terrains*. Teachers are some of the most territorial mammals on this planet. How many of us write our names on every piece of furniture, equipment, material, and piece of flotsam in our proximity? Many of us like to take ownership of a particular subject area, seat in the lounge, or even our favorite place to park. Defaulting to the **They** versus **Us** mentality is sometimes an automatic reaction when we perceive that someone is trying to take something that is ours. But does it help us long term to feel victimized and offended? *Personalizing* adversity only makes it worse as does viewing obstacles as permanent and pervasive. Perhaps we need to do a better job of trying to argue ourselves out of these perceptions.

THE ABCD MODEL

Disputation

Seligman refers to arguing with our thoughts as *disputation*. It's a key practice for building optimism. It works by countering our negative thoughts with deliberation and reflection. To dispute our negative thoughts, we can practice with his ABCD method.

First, we must identify the adversity, our beliefs, and the likely consequences of those beliefs. Next, we must dispute our beliefs and be aware of how different perceptions change the consequences. For example, if we originally explained our adversity with beliefs that are permanent, personal, and pervasive, we feel paralyzed and defeated. Alternately, if we explain our beliefs as temporary, external, and specific, we create hope, which leads to action.

Four Ways to Improve Your Disputation

According to Seligman, there are four ways you can dispute your beliefs more effectively:

> **Evidence**: Ask yourself, "What's the evidence you have for and against the belief?" *(My principal isn't known for making arbitrary decisions. I know that he respects me as a teacher. There have been concerns about the lack of active learning in eighth grade. Perhaps I am being moved there to be a model for the other eighth-grade teachers.)*

Alternatives: Ask yourself, "Is there another way to look at the adversity?" *(If I am totally honest with myself, I've grown a little complacent about my sixth-grade class. I could almost teach physical science in my sleep. Moving to a new area is probably going to help me stay challenged, and I have always performed better when I'm challenged.)*

Implications: Ask yourself, "What's the impact?" Assuming that your negative explanation is right, check whether you are making mountains out of molehills. *(I'm probably not going to like teaching eighth grade as much as I do sixth grade, but I guess at least I will still be teaching middle school science. My first love is middle school, and my second love is science, so this really isn't the end of the world.)*

Usefulness: Ask yourself, "Is this the best time for me to be thinking about this problem?" If now is not the time, then either do something physically distracting, schedule another time with yourself to think things over, or write the negative thoughts down and deal with them when you're ready. *(This assignment change could not have come at a worse time. I have got to have knee surgery in a couple of weeks, I'm trying to study for finals in my graduate courses, and I've got to put my car in the shop this Friday. This is not the best time for me to be thinking about all the changes I will have to make next year. I think I'll put those thoughts on hold for a few weeks until the rest of my life settles down a bit.)*

Other Strategies for Disputation Include

- Reminding yourself that **thoughts aren't facts**

- Identifying **extreme language** (e.g., I will *always* feel this way; things will *never* get better) and rephrasing with less extreme words

- **Questioning the assumptions** or biases that led to your interpretation

- Taking on **someone else's perspective** (e.g., If you told someone else about the situation, would they interpret it the same way?)

Disputing your negative thoughts might help you change your perception and influence the consequences of your altered thoughts as follows:

Adversity: You are being switched from teaching sixth-grade physical science to eighth-grade earth science.

Belief: You have no idea why you are being switched, but you feel confident it has nothing to do with you personally. You have really enjoyed teaching sixth-grade physical science, but you are a good teacher and you believe you can learn to do an effective job teaching earth science, too. You have no idea how long this assignment will last, so if you don't like teaching eighth-grade science, you will take steps to get moved back to teaching sixth-grade science.

Consequences: You are curious about why this decision was made and are anxious to speak with your administrator about why you are being moved. You know that you are a team player and will try to accommodate whatever works best for all concerned. You hope you'll learn to like teaching eighth-grade earth science as much as you do sixth-grade physical science. You are already thinking of some resources you can tap to help you get started.

You may be thinking, "Well, it's easy to list all those steps, but can we really control our thoughts that way?" We believe we can all control our thoughts. It's not always an easy or even a smooth process, but with practice, it can become a habit. We can start reclaiming our joy in teaching by becoming aware of the power we have to control our reactions.

Action Step 2.5

LEARN HOW TO REFRAME ANY SITUATION

Fran Excell's website, How to Reframe Any Situation, offers a 13.5-minute podcast or YouTube video (your choice) with more on the topic of changing the way we look at things. Scan QR Code 2.5 for further explanation and examples.

Competence

One's optimism is largely determined by the degree to which a person feels able to influence desired outcomes. Part of self-determination theory deals with *competence.* The more competent an individual feels, the more likely they are to enjoy their job.

> *Self-belief does not necessarily ensure success, but*
> *self-disbelief assuredly spawns failure.*
>
> —Bandura (1997, p. 77).

In many ways, the opposite of learned helplessness is what Albert Bandura calls *self-efficacy*. Bandura (1989) refers to competence and self-belief as *self-efficacy*. Perceived self-efficacy refers to one's impression of what one is capable of doing. Self-efficacy comes from a variety of sources, such as personal accomplishments and failures, watching others who are similar to oneself, and verbal persuasion from valued others. Bandura is quick to point out that verbal persuasion may temporarily convince us that we should try or should avoid some tasks, but in the final analysis, it is our direct or vicarious experience with success or failure that will most strongly influence our self-efficacy. For example, a beginning of the year Rah-Rah Conclave may temporarily inspire teachers, but their enthusiasm will be short-lived if their job requirements are completely beyond their ability or their perceived beliefs that they can do well.

Bandura explains how important it is to focus on the two things over which each of us always has control—**our choices** and **our efforts**. He maintains that those two concepts are the keys to earned success. When we believe that through our efforts, we can get markedly better at anything we deliberately practice and that our circumstances are largely determined by the choices we make, we become acutely aware of the amount of power we have over our destiny.

People with high-perceived self-efficacy try more, accomplish more, and persist longer at a task than people with low-perceived self-efficacy. Bandura (1986) speculates that this is because people with high-perceived self-efficacy tend to feel they have more control over their environment and, therefore, experience less uncertainty.

So how do we go about increasing our self-efficacy? Part of the answer lies in the research done by attribution theorists. In examining why people think they either were or were not successful in achieving their goals, researchers found that all the rationales and explanations people offered basically fell into four categories. Subjects believed their success or lack of it was mainly dependent one of these four things:

• The difficulty of the task

• The innate ability or talent of the participant

- The luck or fate involved
- The effort extended

Look again at these factors. One of them is different from the others in an important way. Do you see which one? Three of these have to do with external forces, things over which individuals have no control. People cannot control the difficulty of their life challenges. They did not get to pick which or how much natural talent and ability they were born with. And despite what compulsive gamblers believe, no one controls luck. The only one among the four factors over which a person has direct influence is **effort**.

It is both disconcerting and empowering to realize that most of our present situations are shaped by the choices we made and the amount of focused effort we were willing to put forth. People with a high degree of self-efficacy have developed the ability required to implement Seligman's ABCD Model. They are less likely to personalize adversity or see it as permanent or pervasive. Self-efficacy helps us to view challenges as temporary and surmountable; it helps us focus on action rather than on blame.

> Take ownership of what goes on in your classroom. If you blame others, nothing with ever change. If it's your problem, you can solve it. Taking charge of your classroom is empowering because it allows you to move forward toward solutions.
>
> —Julia Thompson (as cited by Ferlazzo, 2013)

The Myth of Multitasking

Unfortunately, some educators base their self-efficacy on their ability to perform myriad duties concurrently over long periods of time. We educators take great pride in being able to do more than one thing at a time. We boast that we can take roll, write today's objectives on the board, sign absentee slips, provide hall passes, sell cheerleader ribbons, take up homework, email a parent, text a colleague, fill out an office form, swill a cup of coffee, find a lost textbook, settle a student dispute, take up lunch money, feed the class iguana, focus the LCD projector, check for dress code violations, monitor the hallway, and prepare our anticipatory set for first period simultaneously during the five minutes of homeroom. New teachers are often overwhelmed by the number of menial tasks that must be completed before the first class even begins. They watch veteran teachers seemingly handle dozens of tasks without even breaking stride and wonder if they will ever be able to manage all they have to do. How do they do so many things all at once? The truth is—they don't. Almost no one can effectively and productively manage multiple tasks at the same time.

Research in the past few years clearly indicates that when we attempt to *multitask*, we do our work less effectively and less efficiently. Massachusetts-based psychiatrist, Dr. Hallowell (2007), who specializes in the treatment of attention deficit/hyperactivity disorder, wrote the book, *Crazy Busy*. In it he calls multitasking a "mythical activity in which people believe they can perform two or more tasks simultaneously." He argues that rather than multitasking, individuals are, in fact, multi-switching among undertakings. He explains that the more the brain has to think about and make decisions about a task, the harder it is to make the switch. Several studies have found that multitasking can actually result in us wasting around 20 to 40 percent of our time, depending on what we're trying to do.

LAYERING

Time management consultants often recommend that people use *layering* to get more done in less time. Understand that layering and multitasking are not usually the same thing. If you start your printer printing a lengthy hand-out, set the filter on the fish tank to self-clean for the next thirty minutes, and begin filing papers while you have your phone on hold waiting for a parent to pick up, you are layering and not multitasking. You are getting more than one thing done at a time, but once you hit "print" on the computer, press "clean" on the filter, and have dialed the parent's number, you are getting more than one thing done at a time. However, you are *attentively focusing* only on filing papers. Layering also applies to grouping similar tasks or planning errands to the same location so that you don't lose time retrieving and putting away the same needed supplies or traveling around randomly each time you need something from the office. Layering applies to tasks that are mostly automatic (sharpening pencils, erasing the board, straightening desks, cutting out shapes, etc.) and don't need your conscious attention.

Rubenstein et al. (2001) believe the simple reason that multitasking doesn't work is because we can't focus on more than one task at a time. But we think we can—so we multitask to try and get more done. Imagine trying to write an email to a parent while mediating a dispute between two students. Both tasks involve mental concentration You cannot clearly focus on both tasks at the same time, so your mind gets overloaded as you switch between the two.

Another major downside to multitasking is the effect it has on our stress levels. Dealing with multiple things at once can cause the brain to produce adrenaline and other stress hormones that make us feel "on edge." Over time, the result of this overstimulation can leave us feeling overwhelmed, exhausted, and disoriented. One of the best ways we can help ourselves feel competent and positive is to take control over the way we do the things we are required to do.

Suggestions for *Single-Tasking* at School

1. When you are with students, be fully present with them. Turn off personal email, tweets, Instagram, Facebook, TikTok, Snapchat, and texts. Limit *teacher drama* and save personal matters for another time. Try to leave your home life at home.

2. Clear your workstations of clutter. You don't have to be the King or Queen of Organization, but your life will be easier to manage if you can find the things you need.

3. Learn to delegate jobs to students. You don't have to feed the iguana, sell the cheerleader ribbons, focus the LCD projector, or even write your objectives on the board. Kids can be taught to do those and other tasks (and some of them love to help).

4. Keep a running list of things to do later. You can capture random thoughts on your electronic device or on a pad of paper, but jotting things down allows you to move them out of your present thoughts and concentrate on the task at hand. (Just be sure to check your list at a designated later time.)

5. Try to finish one task before beginning another. The positive momentum of completing a job is energizing, and you will end up saving time.

© Silver (2015)

Basically, what we are saying is that each of us has the power over our choices and our efforts. We can work to change our thoughts, and we can help those around us learn to be positive and optimistic. Optimism is a learned thought pattern that is not inherent, is not simple, and is not easy. But optimism is achievable, and it is important for us as educators to consciously develop our autonomy, our competence, and our relatedness. Read more on relatedness in Chapter 7: Building a Positive Shared School Community.

1. Do you agree with the authors that people learn to be helpless? Do you think helplessness can be *unlearned*? Give examples to support your beliefs.

2. What's the one thing you can do differently today to let go of control of something that is presently causing you way too much stress?

3. How willing are you to accept responsibility for your circumstances? Give one or two examples of when you were able to attribute your success or failure to something over which you had direct control. How did that affect your next step?

4. Give examples of each of these negative thought patterns you see in yourself or in others.

   Nonproductive thought patterns include the following:

   a. Taking everything personally

   b. Downplaying positive events

   c. Feeling like a victim who is helpless

   d. Expecting the worst

   e. Focusing on the negatives

   f. All-or-nothing thinking

   g. Believing that feelings are facts

   h. Drawing big conclusions with little or no evidence

5. Think of a recent issue that was upsetting to you as a teacher. Apply Seligman's ABCD Model to what happened. Discuss how this model could be helpful to you or to other teachers.

6. Explain any research you have read about multitasking. Do you agree that multitasking on anything except noncognitive tasks is impossible? Why or why not?

7. Describe a situation in which you were multitasking to the nth degree. How did you feel while it was going on? How effectively did you

complete each task? Do you think you saved time in the long run doing more than one thing at a time? Why or why not?

8. Make an argument for *single-tasking* when students are present in the classroom. How is layering different?

9. List three uncontrollable issues affecting your school that bother you. Estimate the amount of time you and others at your school worry or talk about them weekly. What are some ways you can *go around* the issues and keep moving forward?

Action Steps for School Leaders

1. If your staff wants to learn more about how to combat "learned helplessness" in students and the power of mindsets on learning, you and your staff can do a book study on Silver's (2021) book, *Fall Down 7 Times, Get Up 8: Raising and Teaching Self-Motivated Learners, K–12.*

2. With your staff, brainstorm an ABCD Model of dealing with a current school issue.

3. Show one of the videos in this chapter about reframing and lead a discussion on how that might look for your school.

4. Surprise your teachers by taking something off their plates instead of adding to them. Find something teachers are required to do that is not really that important or a program that hasn't been all that successful and announce that you are striking that procedure or program. They will love you for it.

5. Do everything within your power to accommodate a teacher's request for adjusting the temperature in their room. Telling them, "There's no way you can be hot," doesn't help. An exceedingly uncomfortable room temperature (hot or cold) is stressful and makes the person feel helpless.

6. Encourage staff to dress professionally but give them latitude on their choice of attire. Give them permission to wear comfortable shoes (even athletic shoes). Nothing is so tiring as wearing dressy, uncomfortable clothing and shoes all day.

7. When speaking informally with teachers, ask them the same set of questions (i.e., "Where do you want our school to be in five

(Continued)

(Continued)

years?" "What is the most frustrating part of being a staff member in this school?"). Compare and contrast answers to look for larger concerns.

8. At every opportunity, demonstrate how much you value your teachers' time. Keep meetings sparse and short. Allow adequate time for teachers to plan and prep at the beginning of the year as well as between grading periods.

9. Don't hesitate to empathize with teachers as you emphasize the things that are beyond your power to control. Let them know you would change things if you could and you will work with them on ways to reframe their thinking as well as circumvent officious state and district mandates.

10. Until proven otherwise, always assume a positive intent on behalf of your teachers and staff.

DO SOMETHING POSITIVE

When it is obvious that the goals cannot be reached,
don't adjust the goals, adjust the action steps.

—Confucius

As we stated in Chapter 2, we generally can't control the outcome of things. While that is true, we *CAN* control our efforts to make things happen. Dale Carnegie once said, "Action breeds confidence and courage. If you want to conquer fear, do not sit home and think about it. Go out and get busy." We are all familiar with the phrase, "paralyzed by fear." But in addition to fear, other factors can stop a person from acting: a feeling of helplessness, a sense of hopelessness, frustration, fatigue, disillusionment, anger, revenge, not knowing where to start, a feeling of being overwhelmed, a sense of futility. There are many reasons teachers stop acting in the best interest of their students. Some are valid, but none are acceptable.

How many of us have had or have known teachers who retired long before they left the classroom? Administrators, too, sometimes meet various challenges with responses like, "Well, if we can wait this out, I'm going to be retiring in three years anyway." If we (the authors) were independently wealthy people, we would pay those folks to go home now because we know not much positive is happening for the students under their watch. No matter what the cause, inaction can lead to fatalism, complacency, inattention, negativity, pessimism, isolationism, and boredom. Inaction is a clear signal that the person is no longer willing to take a risk or learn anything new. If we don't act, we fail by default and can't even learn from the experience.

For that reason, we believe that it is not enough merely to want to improve or to waste time rationalizing how the system has made it impossible to do our jobs. The best and most productive approach is to *DO* something—anything we think is in the best interest of our ultimate purpose. Even if we make a mistake, doing something brings with it a certain kind of strength. Making a plan, sticking to it, and analyzing the results is energy restoring. Teachers need to remember that maybe we can't do everything for kids but we can do *something*. It's fine to start small. Reach out to just one child. Or try a new teaching strategy with just one class. The point is to start. Doing challenging tasks brings a sense of excitement as well as a sense of accomplishment.

Writing Letters to Students

One year during February, Debbie was feeling a bit disconnected from her students. She felt depressed and disengaged. Her classroom culture was not where she wanted it to be, and she knew she had been distracted by challenges outside of school. She decided to try something different. Normally on Valentine's Day, she signed a commercial Valentine card for each of her fourth graders and attached it to a piece of candy. That year she took extra time and wrote a personal letter to each of her students telling them her favorite things about them. She noticed that as she reflected on the strengths of each student and the individual joys they brought to her, her mood changed dramatically. She felt calmer, more grateful, and more energized. She could barely wait to pass out the Valentine's cards with a personal letter from her tucked inside. Her students were elated. The entire room environment became more hospitable and cordial. Doing that one thing had all kinds of positive effects.

Not one to lose the meaning of the lesson, she made it a priority to write at least one letter to every student every single year from that point forward (not that easy when she moved to middle school and taught over 150 kids a day). Even now, she continues to hear from former students who tell her they still have their letter(s) from her. It was a single act that led to a richer, more meaningful career. We are not saying that every teacher needs to write every student. Debbie happens to be a person with a strength and a passion for writing, so it made sense for her to do what she did. We think every educator has their own talents and preferences and should put those to use. The point is, it's important to act—to try new things. It's empowering when our acts succeed and instructive when they don't. For tips on writing to students, see Appendix 3.1.

> *We may not always be able to reach every student, but we must reach **for** every student.*
>
> —Scott Sater, teacher, Shakopee, MN

Action Rejuvenates Us

There is a kind of inertia involved in both action and inaction. Inaction tends to reinforce itself with more inactivity. On the other hand, action tends to invigorate individuals and perpetuate more action. Effective educators accept that obstacles may slow us down, but they will not stop us. We are the only ones who can stop ourselves permanently. The best way to move toward our purpose is decisively to do those things we can in order to help our students and our fellow educators.

Barbara Blackburn agrees. She recommends that teachers do at least one positive, purposeful action every day. She believes the one action will inspire us to do two, then three, until we are on a roll and just can't stop ourselves.

> You are the thermometer for your classroom; your students' temperatures rise or fall based on what they see happening with you. Find the energy to make those extra efforts with your students. Your energy, excitement, and enthusiasm will drive the levels of your students. Make the decision to take one action every day to positively impact your students:
>
> ✳ Smile today, even if you don't feel like it.
>
> ✳ Find your quietest students and ask about their days.
>
> ✳ Say something positive about your worst student.
>
> ✳ Refuse to allow "I can't" to be uttered by anyone, including yourself. (Blackburn, 2022)

In writing an article about how educators can rejuvenate themselves during the summer months, Silver (2013) writes, "Plan something new for next school year. Focus on something novel for the upcoming school session. Think about a positive aspect of your job you want to enhance or rebuild or something you have been wanting to try. Pick a project that reignites your enthusiasm for teaching and direct your efforts towards something you can look forward to." In other words, the best way we can revive our spirits is to focus on something we can control and deliberately enact steps to empower ourselves toward that end.

One of the greatest gifts we can give our mental, spiritual, and physical well-being is compassionately to let go of the things beyond our control. Instead of wringing our hands with "if only" statements, we can start framing our thoughts around "I can" statements.

IF ONLY . . .	I CAN . . .
My colleagues weren't so negative.	Keep myself healthy and upbeat. I can try to be more encouraging and less judgmental.
The principal had given me the class assignment I wanted.	Learn all I can about this new assignment and approach it as a challenge rather than a punishment.
The "powers that be" would stop making these ridiculous mandates.	Express my concerns in a thoughtful, cogent manner to those who can influence the decisions.
These parents would get more involved.	Communicate with parents in every way possible and actively try to build relationships in which they feel more trusting and inclined to respond.

We can't control the things that have already happened. We *can* control what we do in the present. What is done is done, and how we deal with the outcome is the most important thing. Apportioning blame, either to ourselves or others, is not helpful. It's easy to say, "This is what I should have done," or to lament, "If only I had _____," but the event is over. Hindsight is only good for learning and helping us grow. We must move forward. No matter what happened, look at tomorrow for exactly what it is—a new day with a chance for us to try again. Keep choosing optimism!

Just Keep Moving Forward

- Can't write a letter to every student? Write to one student.

- Can't face cleaning and reorganizing your room? Clean one corner.

- Can't call the ten parents you need to contact? Call one.

- Can't manage to get to school early every day? Pick one day a week to arrive early.

- Can't face learning all the new technology? Learn to do one new thing.

If you're at 0 percent, any gain you make is positive. Always look for the things you CAN do and do them. Action leads to more action. Small gains lead to bigger gains. Actively do something (anything) positive toward your goal. Choose optimism!

LEARN ABOUT THE SCIENCE OF TAKING ACTION

Scan QR Code 3.1 and watch Steve Garguilo's 9.5-minute TEDx Talk, *The Science of Taking Action*. Think about something your team or your school needs to stop thinking about and start DOING. Consider how "action storming" could help in getting things kicked off.

Getting Things Done in Your School and District

In her article, "Getting Things Done in Your School District," Strasser (2022) provides excellent suggestions for getting things done at the school or district level. She tells educators that sometimes we need to be a PITA (yes, it does stand for what you think it does). She says that other people's frustration or annoyance with our dogged quest should not derail us from moving toward our purpose. Their irritation with our relentless pursuit of a solution should not thwart our persistence. Without implying they lack competence, we should let people know we recognize that a situation may require "elevation" on their overpacked radar. She recommends that sometimes we need to employ a lateral carpet bomb approach (e.g., She once wrote an email and sent it to virtually everyone even slightly involved that began, "This is an email to many, many people. I am hoping to glean some insight."). Her belief is that someone would likely be able to provide some clarity or suggestions to help her get going again. Strasser also advises educators to know who really runs things:

> That would generally be the following people: the nurse; the secretaries; the custodians; and the bus drivers. Make an intentional, deliberate effort to call these folks by their names, buy them donuts, and otherwise recognize them for their often-unseen work. You would be amazed at what a secretary can do that your boss—or you, for that matter—cannot. If you're consistently kind to them, they will move mountains for you. And you should be anyway.

Strasser reminds us that asking for help is easier when we show goodwill and use the three most powerful sentences in the English language: "I don't know." "I need help." "I'm sorry." When all else fails, Strasser says, you sometimes just have to do it yourself. She tells the story of a student in her school who lived in a house with a broken heater. Temperatures one night were dropping into the negative numbers. "While we investigate federal programs for energy assistance, which is a long and complicated process, she now has two space heaters provided by—you guessed it—her teachers." Strasser's team demonstrated the adage that we can't control what happens to other people, but we can control how we show up for them when things get hard.

And finally, Strasser recommends that teachers refrain from equating setbacks or rejections with failing. She suggests we view taking action to overcome barriers as a game rather than taking rebuffs as a personal affront.

> It helps me think of my roadblocks the way my kids think of levels in a video game. You're going to encounter "bosses," and some of those will be bigger and badder than others. None of them will play fair.

> But there's nothing like gamifying a challenge to help leach the pain, frustration, and self-doubt out of it; and as a video game will show you, there's no other way to move beyond the level than continuing, with cheer and good will, to fight the boss. A game does not think you're evil, incompetent, bad, or wrong. Don't take it personally. Just keep going. (Strasser, 2022)

Be Careful About Overloading Plates

Action and momentum are powerful means to stimulate optimism but only if we carefully moderate our expectations. Setting out to tackle an unreasonable task load will quickly extinguish motivation and drive. Much like Lev Vygotsky's zone of proximal development theory, we need to avoid the space where the task load is excessively demanding as well as eschew an operating mode filled with only mundane, non-challenging tasks. The optimal goal is to trim policies and procedures to give educators a chance to function in a zone that energizes by allowing us time to try new things.

In his book, *De-implementation: Creating the Space to Focus on What Works*, former principal, DeWitt (2022), offers an idea for setting a purpose for professional development keynotes and workshops. At the end of the presentation, DeWitt suggests you ask participants to engage in the following activity.

Don't Overload Your Plates

- Take a paper plate and write down the new strategies you just promised yourself you would implement in your classrooms.

- Take your plate home and look at what you wrote.

- Cross out three of the strategies you wrote down.

DeWitt believes that the strategies that are left are those the educator is most likely to commit to. It's a great reminder that we need to try new ideas but also be cautious about overloading our plates. Too many required tasks or undertakings that are far beyond our present competency level can have a debilitating effect on our attitude and our bodies.

Taking Positive Steps With Our Health

Part of the criticism about toxic positivity during the COVID pandemic and beyond is the constant mantra from school leaders that teachers should get better about self-care. No kidding? How were we supposed to take this seriously in a time of teacher shortages, negative public scrutiny, and more undertakings than ever piled on our plates? It seems we are being told that not only is it our fault there are serious "learning gaps" from the past two plus years, but we should also be ashamed for not taking better care of ourselves.

A few leaders and districts are making concrete moves to help teachers invest in their personal wellness (gym memberships, healthier food options, health fairs on campus, and health experts teaching classes to staff), but for many, the whole movement feels like using platitudes to mask deeper issues.

We address stress and mental health in Chapter 5, but in keeping with this chapter's focus on doing positive things, we offer some concrete suggestions for healthy choices to work on now. We realize that we are writing about things that most of you already know. Our attempt is not so much to *inform* you as to *remind* you how important you and your health are. We hope you will be able to relate to what we are saying, remember to take care of yourself, and initiate some positive steps toward your well-being. (And it's okay if you smile at some of our irreverent examples.)

One of the criticisms of Western culture is that we tend to ignore even very clear signals that our body sends. Rather than in the Eastern way of "Eat when you're hungry, sleep when you're tired," we try to regulate our meals and bedtimes with what is dictated by our schedules or the clock. We say things like, "I can't be hungry; it's only 10:30 a.m." "I can't possibly be sleepy; it's only 8:30 p.m., and I've got way too much to do to go to bed now." We have learned to turn a deaf ear to messages from our bodies.

Scientists tell us that our body sends us very clear messages when we are not meeting its needs. Different people have various reactions to a body in need of help, but these are just some of the ways our bodies try to warn us: headaches, irritability, fatigue, feelings of hopelessness, depression, anxiety, boredom, ulcers, frequent colds, sleeplessness or too sleepy, pain in neck and back, pain in joints and muscles, weight gain or weight loss, cardiovascular problems, gastrointestinal problems, high blood pressure, absenteeism, apathy, disregard for appearance, lack of energy, mood swings, paranoia, increased use of drugs or alcohol, and loss of sense of humor. Do you recognize any of these signals? Are you aware of when your body tries to alert you that it is in trouble? (WARNING: If you find that you are presently experiencing ALL of these symptoms, put this book down immediately and head to an emergency room! You are in Big Trouble.)

In a career that often requires us to be selfless, many teachers see themselves as healers and fixers. We get so busy taking care of everyone else that we often neglect our own welfare. Too many times, we put our own needs last and tend to think of those who put effort into taking care of their physical, psychological, spiritual, mental, and social needs as being a bit self-absorbed and even selfish. Nothing could be further from the truth. Burning the candle at both ends will eventually lead to complete and total burnout, and we have too many excellent teachers leaving the field already. **Taking care of oneself is probably the least selfish thing a teacher can do.**

> *A man too busy to take care of his health is like a mechanic too busy to take care of his tools.*
>
> —Spanish proverb

You Are What You Eat

No one reading this chapter needs a lecture on healthy eating. Every educated person is regularly inundated with information about what constitutes wise decisions on food and beverage choices. Advertisers make sure we are aware of the latest and greatest food products that promote health and longevity. Knowing is not the problem. Doing is the problem.

Recently, we had lunch with a rather "robust" colleague who was finishing a huge carb-laden meal with a piece of coconut cream pie topped with a scoop of ice cream. (We're not judging.) She suddenly swooned a bit then said, "Oh my, you guys may have to take me to the emergency room. I have diabetes, and I think I've just knocked my insulin level totally out of whack." What? We looked at each other with open mouths. Obviously, we stopped what we were doing and took her to the hospital, but we were not happy. When did it become our responsibility to rescue her from her own poor decisions? It turned out that she was okay, but the whole incident made us think really hard about personal responsibility.

Rational human beings who drive cars put fuel in them so that they will run. Most of us are selective about what kind of fuel we put in our vehicles (or at least we *were* selective before fuel prices shot out of control). We know that higher grades of gasoline may cost a little more but will be better for our auto in the long run. We realize that input generally equals performance. But when it comes to our bodies, we sometimes forget that food is supposed to be fuel that helps us perform at our best. Skipping meals, eating low nutrient snacks, or indulging in food or drinks we know are detrimental to our short-term performance or long-term endurance is just not smart. And if we choose to make choices that are less than brainy, the least we can do is take responsibility for our choices.

Whose Responsibility Is This?

Our infamous curmudgeon, Ms. Culsmucker, enters the lounge on a Monday morning griping and complaining because she woke up late, had bus duty, and had no chance to eat breakfast. She is cranky and upset because she knows she will have to spend lunch grading the papers she didn't get to last night, so she's already projecting what a horrid day it is going to be. Suddenly, she spies a huge cake purchased in honor of all faculty members with birthdays this month. She grabs a large corner piece with extra icing, scarfs it down, and polishes it off with approximately a half liter of punch. Can you predict what she is going to be like in about fifteen minutes when all that sugar hits her system? She is going to be like a mosquito on speed. Before first period is over, she will write fifteen referrals, chew out her aide, and dash off a vile email to all the parents blaming them for procreating in the first place. And of course, by the time her afternoon classes are scheduled to begin, she will be barely able to put one foot in front of the other. She will blame all her woes on the students, their parents, her colleagues, her administrators, the school, and anyone but herself. Maybe it is time for a chat about personal responsibility.

We believe that teachers should be aware of their personal body needs and take care of them. Whether you are someone who thrives on the largely carbohydrate fare served in the lunchroom or one who needs several small protein-rich snacks spread out throughout the day, make it happen. As far as we know, teachers are not required to eat what others prepare. If you have lunchroom duty, you can still take your own food with you. If you need to keep fruit or a protein snack cold, put a refrigerator in your room. (Yes, we know some schools do not allow that. So get one and hide it . . . er . . . bring a small ice chest, carry an insulated lunch bag, or make friends with the human ecology teacher and use her fridge.) The point is, take care of yourself!

Many schools now offer wellness programs for their teachers. Even if you're not lucky enough to have such a program, you can usually find a colleague who shares your interest in good nutrition and can swap turns bringing healthy snacks, remind you about your goals, and encourage you when it's a *Need for Chocolate Day*. It isn't so much about losing weight to look better as it is about being the weight you need to be to do your personal best. Forget about the scale, pant size, or the mirror; just decide to make it part of your daily routine to eat foods that are right for you and limit those that are not. It takes lots of energy to be an effective teacher, and optimism is fueled by food as well as the mind.

Stay Hydrated

Sometimes, we have to laugh at the irony in our jobs. During the shelter-in-place mandate, a lot of us were thrilled because for the first time in our careers we could go to the bathroom any time we wanted. Just one problem—there was no longer any toilet paper! Now we are back to plenty of toilet paper but no time to take a potty break.

Readers are no doubt aware of the research on drinking plenty of water throughout the day. Although we are big proponents of drinking pure water (easier on the bladder and kidneys), the main idea is to take in enough fluids of any kind to keep the body hydrated. Juice, sodas, coffee, tea, energy drinks, and even some foods count toward getting enough fluid. (And as teachers, we all know, "caffeine is our friend.")

A mere 2 percent drop in body fluids can lead to the inability to focus on a computer screen, trouble with concentration, and fuzzy math (we thought we were bad at arithmetic, but now we know we were just thirsty). Dehydration is the number one cause of afternoon fatigue, and bodies can become dehydrated long before we feel thirst. Both educators and their students need to drink plenty of fluids throughout the school day to remain mentally alert and at their physical best. Yes, we know that if you drink a lot of water during the day, it's going to mean lots of restroom breaks—so plan accordingly.

Action Step 3.2

GET HEALTHY: HYDRATION

For more information about healthy hydration, scan QR Code 3.2 to watch this short video from NBC News Learn, *Get Healthy: Hydration*. (Caution: It may send you running to the bathroom to check the color of your pee.)

The bottom line is this: If you want to stay positive and joyful, you must take good care of yourself. Eat right and drink plenty of fluids (preferably pure water). No surprise there.

Exercise: "I Can't Run Because I Spill My Drink"

Not only is it recommended that humans get regular cardio-vascular exercise (aerobics, running, swimming, etc.), but as we age, we are advised to include regular strength resistant and anaerobic workouts. Doctors tell us that nearly every medical condition and ailment can be improved with regular exercise. That includes cancer, diabetes, heart problems, arthritis, immune deficiencies, common colds, joint pain, insomnia, high blood pressure, dementia, depression, and more. Exercise is one of the simplest and most direct ways to improve our attitudes as well as our physical health. So why do people avoid it?

Many of us equate exercise with the nightmare of being back in seventh-grade gym class with a PE teacher who made Hannibal Lecter look like Mr. Rogers. The teacher was not happy until you were drenched in sweat and writhing in pain from a lengthy round of calisthenics. At that point, they would smirk and say, "I don't think you're trying. Let's start again." The thought of exercise conjures up all kinds of painful memories (literally and figuratively). We see our more athletic friends wearing their "I Run for Life" T-shirts as we proudly brandish our "I Run for No One" XXXL stretchy sweats. We snarl, "It's all about genetics, and my genes are just fluffy," as we avoid all exercise except pulling up the lever on our recliners.

There is not time nor space here to address all the excuses from teachers about why we don't exercise. You may hear yourself saying, "Oh no, I missed going to the gym today . . . that makes five years in a row." But we are all more than aware it is impossible to think about taking care of ourselves without considering a regular, sustainable exercise plan.

Again, many schools offer exercise sessions, weight room availability, and innovative programs such as Zumba, CrossFit, high-intensity interval training (HIIT), or even pickleball for their teachers. Whether our school does or does not offer wellness opportunities, it is up to us as individuals to take responsibility for taking care of our bodies. Our wonderful spirits won't survive long without a suitable place to reside. Even if you are so out of shape you can barely stand, you can do chair exercises (available on video) until you are strong enough to go to the next level.

Many times, people think that to start exercising means to jump in and "go for the gold." That's only if you want to be sure you won't keep it up. Instead of "going for the gold," we believe you should go for the beige or pink or chartreuse or whatever represents one step ahead of where you are now. Start small. Park a little further away at school or at the mall just to make sure you walk further. Take the stairs more times that you have to. Practice holding in your stomach as tightly as you can between classes. Walk around your classroom constantly instead of standing, sitting, or propping yourself against something. Bend over from the waist to retrieve items (real or imaginary) from the floor. Stretch every chance you get.

And most importantly, don't wait for the chance to regularly exercise (at least thirty minutes three times a week), *make* the chance. Make it a priority. Write it into your schedule. Get an exercise partner who will hold you accountable. Pick a time that works for you. If you're a morning person, do it then. You can also squeeze it in at lunch, just after school, or sometime in the evening. It's just a matter of preference.

And here's the good news: You don't have to run or do calisthenics if you don't want to. You don't have to buy a treadmill or join an aerobics class if that's not your preference. You just have to do something—anything. You can do yourself just as much good with regular fast-paced walking through your neighborhood as running around a track. You can dance yourself into fitness, skate yourself into better shape, or play certain sports to get into good condition. It's really a matter of figuring out what you find most appealing and doing it regularly. You don't need fancy exercise apparel. In most cases, you don't need specialty shoes or expensive equipment. You just need to realize that your energy, your optimism, and your health are influenced by the choices you make. It is an individual responsibility. As Nike says, "Just DO it."

THE MAID STUDY AND PLACEBO EFFECT ON FITNESS

Scan QR Code 3.3 to watch this 1-minute video, *The Maid Study and Placebo Effect on Fitness* and think about what ideas teachers can take from it.

In 2007, a Harvard psychologist, Dr. Elllen Langer, conducted a study including eighty-eight hotel maids. She told forty-four of the maids that their daily jobs involved serious exercise and educated them on how their daily tasks contributed to their physical fitness. She told the other forty-four maids nothing. After one month, she found that the maids who had been told they exceeded the surgeon general's guidelines for fitness had lost weight, lowered their blood pressure, and developed a healthier body composition—despite no changes to their diet or daily routine. The control group, however, saw none of these benefits. It seems that just being attentive to the amount of exercise we do in our regular jobs can help our bodies get healthier (Crum, 2007).

Depending on your job, look at all the ways you move throughout the day. Granted, high school coaches are generally called to exercise more than high school English teachers, and primary teachers are usually far more active in class than middle school math teachers. But we all move. Why not analyze our daily movement requirements and start viewing them as great body activities rather than as "just part of the job."

Action Step 3.4

PHYSICAL ACTIVITY MINDFULNESS CHECKLIST

1. List the various ways you are required to move your body during a normal school day. Do you have to bend and stretch to assist learners? Do you have to climb stairs? How many steps do you take during a normal school day?

2. Study how activity might affect your body. Check a fitness app to see how many calories you are burning and which muscle groups you are targeting. Fill in a chart at the end of each day delineating exactly how much physical activity you performed in doing your job.

3. Start making a mental link between each task and the benefits you hope to see. For instance, when you are walking upstairs, imagine your quads and glutes engaging with each

(Continued)

(Continued)

step. When you squat to assist a seated student, picture what is happening to your glutes, thighs, hips, and legs.

4. Try to view trips to the office, teacher workroom, cafeteria, and playground as opportunities to accumulate steps for the day.

5. Picture your daily routines and envision how your actions are contributing to your improved body movement.

Teachers are human. Teacher time and energy are finite resources. Kids deserve teachers who will work tirelessly to help them reach their full potential. They also deserve a mentally healthy teacher who wants to be in the room with them and has the emotional reserves to show compassion when they need it. This means that—despite what the movies suggest—it is actually counterproductive for teachers to take a second job to buy books or pull all-nighters planning field trips. It also means that schools and districts should plan around using teacher time and energy wisely.

—Roxanna Elden, NBCT teacher, speaker, and author

Sleep Is Not Just for Slackers

Experts recommend seven to eight hours of sleep for most every night (Van Dongen et al., 2003). Teachers often chuckle when we tell them that. They protest that they can't do all they need to do in their lives if they sleep that much. They tell us that to make a living, they need to be awake for at least eighteen to nineteen hours a day. Our answer is simple—you probably won't be living much longer if you keep that up.

Sometimes, people equate the need for sleep with some sort of weakness, an indicator of laziness, or just an excuse to get out of doing things. That's indeed unfortunate because people who go without regular restorative sleep are asking for all kinds of mental and health problems. Studies have documented the negative effect of sleep deprivation on memory, reaction time, comprehension, and attention. Even physical and emotional states can be affected.

Why It's Important to Get Sufficient Quality Sleep

1. **It helps your body defend against disease.**

   Poor sleep can increase inflammation, blood pressure, insulin resistance, and cardiovascular disease, as well as decrease blood sugar regulation. Proper sleep can fight cardiovascular disease, diabetes, and intracellular pathogens, like flu, HIV, and cancer. (Pratt, 2019)

2. **It improves memory and concentration.**

   Getting enough high-quality sleep promotes memory, problem-solving ability, creativity, emotional processing, and judgment. There is evidence that improving sleep can boost both short- and long-term cognitive performance. Better sleep can reduce the likelihood of age-related cognitive decline. (Suni, 2022)

3. **It regulates metabolism and weight.**

   Lack of sleep hampers our metabolism and contributes to weight gain. Too little sleep triggers a cortisol spike. This stress hormone signals our bodies to conserve energy for the purpose of fueling our waking hours (so our bodies hang on to fat). Sleepy brains can crave high calorie snacks and sometimes lack the impulse control to say no to unhealthy food choices. (Paturel, 2022)

4. **It enhances alertness.**

   Too little sleep can impede clear thinking, interfere with learning, and hurt performance. Sleepiness slows down our thought processes and makes it difficult to focus and pay attention. Big dangers with excessive sleepiness are slower reaction times and drowsiness, which can lead to fatigue-related accidents. (Peri, 2021)

5. **It elevates moods.**

   Sleep deficiency and mood disorders are closely linked. Sleep loss can affect our moods (and vice versa). "Studies show people who are sleep deprived report increases in negative moods (anger, frustration, irritability, sadness) and decreases in positive moods." (Better Health Channel, n.d.)

6. **It Increases libido.**

   (We knew this one would get your attention!) Seriously, research has shown that lack of sleep can have serious consequences on our sex lives. Lack of sleep may also lead to sexual issues like a lower desire for sex, infertility, and erectile dysfunction. Improving the amount and quality of our sleep can boost our libidos. (Hall, 2021)

Everyone's individual sleep needs vary. In general, most healthy adults are built for sixteen hours of wakefulness and need an average of eight hours of sleep a night. However, some individuals can function without sleepiness or drowsiness after as little as six hours of sleep. Others can't perform at their peak unless they've slept ten hours (Van Dongen et al., 2003).

Many times, sleep disorder starts with a physiological reason. More and more teachers tell us that either they or their significant other snores loudly or suffers from the much more serious condition of sleep apnea. Since Debbie has had sleep apnea for over thirty years, we are quite familiar with its ramifications. It is a destructive and sometimes deadly condition in which during sleep, a person stops breathing for as long as a minute and then gasps desperately for air. This happens over and over during the sleep cycle, and the apnea sufferer never fully wakes up or fully gets REM sleep. It disrupts the sleep of not only the sufferer but also of anyone within earshot of the snorting, gasping person with the apnea.

Apnea, like most sleep disorders, is treatable. Most people have at least heard of a device called the C-PAP machine, which has proven to be highly effective in the treatment of apnea. Unfortunately, some people assume that if they go to a sleep doctor, they will automatically be consigning themselves to a lifetime using a sleep machine at night. C-PAP machines are always being updated and modified to make them more user-friendly, and many people find them to be quite comfortable and virtually nonintrusive.

Also, the machine is not the only option to dealing with apnea. We recommend that anyone who has or suspects they have a sleep disorder should schedule an appointment with an ear, nose, and throat specialist, a neurologist, or a specialized sleep doctor. If the problem is with the person sharing your bedroom, we advise you to encourage them to at least have the condition checked out. You may want to point out to them that sleep apnea restricts oxygen intake and can permanently enlarge their heart. Look it up and see how serious a health problem it is.

Our bodies have extraordinary ways of telling us when they need to rest, restore, and rejuvenate. Some of us need to listen a little better. Dishes left in the sink, papers not graded, or a TV program unwatched are not as important as one's health. Sleep is not a luxury nor is it self-indulgent. It is a vital part of keeping ourselves fully functioning and ready to be deliberately optimistic. If you are tired, rest. If you are sleepy, go to sleep. Be creative and find a way to get in a nap or go to bed at a reasonable time.

IMPLEMENT SLEEP HACKS

For tips on how to best achieve restorative sleep, scan QR Code 3.5 to watch the 3-minute video, *5 Sleep Hacks for a Deep Restorative Sleep:*

Commit to using the hacks you think will work for you.

Be Proactive: Get Annual Check-Ups

Regularly see your physician, your optometrist, your dentist, your dermatologist, and any specialist you need to see. Pap smears, mammograms, colonoscopies, skin biopsies, other regular tests can save your life or certainly improve the quality of it. Like us, you probably can name some important people in your circle who are gone too soon from this earth simply because they failed to get the kinds of tests and information they needed in a timely manner. Ask yourself this question, "If I can't make time for the tests, how am I going to make time for the surgeries and treatments I will need because I didn't get tested?"

We can't control all aspects of our health, but we can control the preventative health measures we take. We (the authors) are big believers in educators being proactive rather than reactive. Many times, we can do things preemptively that will significantly "smooth the waters" down the line. The operative phrase here is "do positive things." If you are not yet ready to do great things, do small things in a great way.

●●● DISCUSSION QUESTIONS AND ACTION STEPS

1. Name a time when you tried a new idea, and it worked so well that you are still doing it. Do your regularly try new things? Why or why not?

2. Have you or one of your offspring ever received a positive letter from a teacher or mentor? How did it make you feel? Do you write notes or letters to your students? Why or why not?

3. Think of a school problem you are currently dealing with. Brainstorm as many creative solutions as you can (don't edit yourself or limit yourself to

(Continued)

(Continued)

traditional ideas). Discuss each proposed solution and decide if it would be worth trying.

4. How does your body let you know when you're under too much stress? Which symptoms described in the chapter apply to you? What do you generally do when you experience those symptoms?

5. Would you recommend your present dietary habits to your students? Why or why not?

6. What reasonable modifications to your present exercise program could you make now that would greatly enhance your fitness by this time next year? Do you think you will make the changes you just listed? Why or why not?

7. Where are you on your recommended health care preventative measures (physicals, dental visits, colonoscopy, mammogram, prostate check, eye check-up, etc.)? If you are behind, what is keeping you from taking care of yourself? Would you tell people you care about to follow your lead? Why or why not?

8. Identify your normal sleep habits and defend their appropriateness for your long-term health goals.

9. List at least five things you do every week just to take care of you. What is your rationale behind doing these things?

Action Steps for School Leaders

1. Plan a retreat before school starts or in January. Make sure it is off campus and is in a desirable location. Mix learning objectives with fun collaborative activities. Provide time for personal reflection.

2. Don't leave letter writing to students to just the teachers. When you see something great happen or hear of a student success or loss, write a personal note.

3. Write notes or letters to teachers to congratulate, encourage, praise, or comfort every time you get a chance. Personal heartfelt notes from leaders are much more valued than a "jeans pass" or "park in the principal's spot for one day" certificates.

4. Arrange for a local masseuse or two to come to school for a day and do chair massages. Staff members can sign up for ten- to fifteen-minute intervals throughout the day. Don't forget to get one yourself.

5. Set up a health fair just for staff members at your school. Have medical people on hand to do blood tests, cholesterol checks, eye screens, blood pressure checks, and whatever else you think would be beneficial to your staff. Also invite dieticians, exercise pros, and other people who work with wellness to set up table and offer free advice and brochures.

6. Invite a sleep expert to present to your faculty about the importance of sleep for them and for the students they teach.

7. Invest in putting a couple of treadmills in the teacher lounge or other accessible area. Sometimes walking helps re-energize people (And fast walking may be a healthy outlet for teachers who are just about to snap!).

8. Investigate getting discount memberships for all staff members to a local health club or exercise facility.

9. Provide healthy snacks and drinks at all faculty meetings, professional development days, parent–teacher nights, and any time teachers are required to be at school beyond the workday. (Of course, you can always supplement healthy snacks with chocolate and other "questionable" treats.)

10. Why not survey the adults at school to ask them what they need to help them with their physical and mental health and then do what is feasible? Maybe a teacher would rather have a standing desk. Perhaps the staff would like to hire a certified yoga instructor to conduct regular sessions (in person or virtually). Possibly a group of teachers would like to reinvent a small space on campus as a "relaxation room." Ask them what they want and need instead of making assumptions or only listening to a chosen few.

OWN YOUR PART

*We can't just row on our own. We need to row together
in the direction of something bigger. I have to talk to you,
I have to learn from you, I have to listen to you, I have
to say difficult truths to you at times, and you to me.*

—Mieliwocki (as cited by Loewus, 2012),
National Teacher of the Year

Time to Speak Up and Speak Out

As presenters, we (the authors) consistently remind educators and educational entities that teachers need more of a voice. We encourage teachers to stand up and be heard. We are starting to see more teacher-generated blogs and articles. We have had the opportunity to listen to teacher presenters who advocate for a larger teacher presence in important decision-making. After all, who is there better to speak about what works best for kids than the people on the frontlines in the classrooms every school day? How can teachers best act as our own advocates?

First, we the educators have to be willing to stop blaming outside factions and bickering among ourselves. We need to acknowledge our collective weaknesses and bring to the forefront our combined strengths. Maybe it is time to stop worrying about who took our *clearly labeled personal* yogurt out of the lounge refrigerator or parked in our favorite parking spot and start dealing with the real issues.

We resent the scrutiny of those outside education who want to micromanage and disrespect our profession, but have we done enough to "police our own ranks?" Have we adequately called each other to task when programs and systems aren't working? Are we willing to reexamine long-established policies and conventional procedures to make way for educators to innovate and try creative solutions? As we stated earlier, autonomy is a fundamental part of feeling optimistic. Taking back our power as professional educators would go a long way in increasing teacher autonomy. To advance this change, we must be willing to hold not only ourselves accountable but also each other.

It is time we become more honest with ourselves and with each other. We realize that educators will confront parents, students, and even our administrators (as long as two people come with us), but most of us hesitate to confront a coworker. We sometimes prefer to let a sleeping dog lie than to speak up. Rather than uniformly going along when one of our colleagues is out of line, we should stand up for what we think is ethically correct. We can't control what other people do, but we can control whether or not we participate in their behavior or enable them.

Action Step 4.1

HALL DUTY—WHAT WOULD YOU DO?

Read the following scenario and think about your most likely response:

Think about the teacher who never is at her door during class change. She finds countless excuses for why she cannot manage to make her way to the hall, even though the administrator has repeatedly told teachers to make it a priority to be there. You and some of the other teachers have complained among yourselves more than once about having to "pick up her slack." Inevitably, the administrator is in the hall during a class change, and she's again not at her door. The administrator asks you and a couple of other teachers if this is her normal routine. You hedge and reply, "We really haven't noticed." The principal walks into her room, discusses the incident, and tells the teacher that she is going to put a note of reprimand in her file. As soon as the administrator departs, Ms. I-Can't-Be-Bothered-With-Hall-Duty rushes to the rest of you in tears wanting to be consoled by her comrades. What do you do?

A. Hug her, dry her tears, and tell her what a horrible, terrible, no good, very bad person the principal is.

B. Assure her that everyone skips hall duty occasionally, and it was just bad luck she got caught.

C. Offer to find a way to alert her the next time an administrator is in the hall.

D. Tell her that you're sorry she got a reprimand but there are several reasons she should be in the hall.

E. Nod politely and walk away quickly.

The most common response we get from teachers is answer "E." Admittedly, that seems to be the easiest course of action, but it doesn't solve anything for anyone. The best thing for everyone is answer "D." All the adults at school need to support one another, but also, we need to hold each other accountable. Positive peer pressure is a compelling impetus for influencing behavior. We don't want to be complicit in allowing the adults at school to do less than their best.

In the preceding scenario, perhaps you and the other teachers could share tips on how you make the time to be at the door during class change. You could express your feelings or even offer research about the importance of the teacher greeting each student as they enter the room. We teachers need to speak up and to challenge each other to do our very best for students in every possible way.

It is also appropriate for teachers to stand up for themselves as staff members. Speaking from the heart has a lot of power. For instance, if none of your colleagues are showing up for hall duty, you might say to them (individually or as a group), "I feel overwhelmed when the rest of you don't come into the hall during transition periods. There are too many students for me to monitor by myself, and with some of these big kids, I get really uncomfortable when I don't have you there for back-up."

We need to be compassionate and kind with each other but, at the same time, be assertive and forthright. It's important that we gently nudge each other to bring our best game to class each day. Larkin (2013) calls candid conversations about how to get better in our teaching an act of *compassionate confrontation*. He says that we should not be as concerned about bruising professional egos as we are about helping each other learn hard truths about our teaching expertise. He thinks the lessons are best learned from trusted colleagues. With a healthy, trusting relationship, perhaps you could expect a conversation like the one that follows.

Bad Teaching Day

A group of history teachers are having an informal gathering in the lounge. It has been a hard day, and everyone is just glad it's over.

Dennis chuckles, "Yeah, I kind of hit a new low today. I was so tired by seventh hour that I just handed the kids a study guide, told them to fill it out, and dared them to say one word. And wouldn't you know it, my two worst boys got into it. I had to write them both up and send them to time-out. Then four of my other students just shut their books and refused to work, so I wrote them up, too. Man, I don't know what is wrong with these kids."

A couple of his colleagues exchange looks. Jaden asks, "You gave them a study guide to fill out for the entire fifty minutes? Seriously? Wow, that doesn't sound like you, Dennis. Usually you have the coolest activities for the kids to do. You're kind of my hero when it comes to engaging kids."

Dennis replies, "I know, but I was tired, and dang it, all I asked was for these kids to just be quiet and work. Is that too much to expect?"

(Continued)

(Continued)

Lyndon chimes in, "Are you talking about that study guide that comes from the book publisher?"

Dennis nods his head sheepishly.

Lyndon is incredulous, "But, Dennis, isn't that the class with lots of kids who can barely read? I mean, I can see how they got off-task if they couldn't read the text."

Dennis shakes his head, "Yeah, I know. It was a lame assignment. I just didn't have anything left in me, you know?"

Reina says gently, "You know, Dennis, I think we've all been there. I know I have. But later, when I thought about how unfair it was to the students, I realized I had to be more in tune with what really works for them. You should have told us you were having a bad day. We would have been glad to step in and help."

Dennis looks around, "So y'all think it was my fault that my kids acted out?"

Jaden responds, "I don't know, Dennis; we weren't there. What do you think?"

Dennis pauses and thinks. He then takes a deep breath and groans, "Yeah, you're right. I knew it wasn't the thing to do when I did it. I was just kind of hoping you all would tell me it's okay."

Lyndon slaps him on the back, "Well, you should have known that wasn't going to happen, Dude. We can't ever let you be less than *Dennis-like*, now, can we?"

Dennis gathers his stuff to leave. He smiles and says, "Looks like I've got some thinking to do this afternoon. See you tyrants tomorrow!"

We all know why holding each other accountable is so difficult; it means we must deal with the toughest problem within our school—the ADULTS. It means that we must look deeply into our biases toward each other, the parents, the administrators, and the kids. Working together, respecting each other, supporting each other, and holding each other accountable is the best way we can help ourselves and ultimately help our students.

Deliberate optimism is not inherent nor is it easy. Dealing with other humans is a tricky business. We need to get to know each other. It helps if we can appreciate each other's backgrounds, experiences, and perspectives. Disagreement is essential to growth, and if we can maintain a respectful norm for solving our differences, we can have the hopeful, helpful adult relationships required to do this incredibly intricate job we do.

Radical Responsibility

Taking ownership of our profession means that we stop excusing, stop blaming, and start taking responsibility. We make decisions based on what is best for students, and we behave with an integrity grounded in a shared value system. We avoid assigning blame because we know it subverts personal growth and creates victims instead of visionaries.

We the teachers need to step up and take responsibility for not only our own classrooms but for every student in our schools. We need to be willing to offer guidance to novice colleagues, work with teachers who are struggling, and learn from teachers more accomplished than we. It is time to let those few incompetent, ineffective colleagues know that we are moving forward and they can join us or get out of the way. We need to listen to parents, community members, and other interested parties with an open mind and an open heart. In addition, we must remind them we are qualified, competent, skilled, professionals who are responsible for the decisions we make about our classrooms.

Action Step 4.2

**ARE YOU TAKING 100 PERCENT OF
YOUR RESPONSIBILITY?**

Scan QR Code 4.2 to watch this 5-minute video from the Conscious Leadership Group. Ask yourself what taking 100 percent responsibility could mean to our profession.

How Do We Take Responsibility for Our Profession?

How do we take responsibility for our profession? How to we maintain realistic optimism in the face of escalating challenges? We begin by believing that we have the power to shape and control what happens in our daily lives. We take responsibility not necessarily for everything that happens to us but over how we respond. The following are ways to help educators choose responsibility.

Tips for Choosing Responsibility

1. **We prioritize ourselves.** Chapter 2 discusses self-efficacy and competence. It is imperative that we as educators develop a sense of self-worth about our abilities and pride in what we have accomplished so far. We need to believe that we are capable, worthy individuals and act that way. As we discuss in Chapters 2, 3, and 5, it is our responsibility to hone our skills, our bodies, and our minds so that we indeed bring our best selves to the classroom.

2. **We stop playing the blame game.** Pointing fingers and casting judgements conveniently keeps us from accepting responsibility (e.g., "If the parents would take more responsibility, we wouldn't have this problem."). When we are hyper-focused on the mistakes or incompetencies of others, we miss the point of lessons to be learned from our own missteps and growth to be made. Taking 100 percent responsibility means not allocating different percentages toward asking, "Who caused this in the first place?" but rather saying, "This situation is what it is, and I'm 100 percent responsible for what I do about it from here."

3. **We take the time for self-reflection.** Self-reflecting is not easy, but it's imperative that we pause and look deeply into our motives, our reactions, and our goals. Questions we need to ask ourselves are the following:

   - What is my goal here? What am I trying to achieve?

   - What is my true motivation? Am I acting out of fear or hurt or anger instead of an intent to do the right thing?

   - Am I making this more about me than the cause I'm supposedly promoting?

   - Am I really giving this purpose my total, focused attention and energy?

   - Am I listening to others with the intent to understand?

4. **We assume accountability.** Misplaced pride is the primary reason people do not take responsibility. We are too proud to admit we made a mistake or even that we are part of the problem. Taking responsibility means we hold ourselves accountable for everything that happens, good or bad, and we learn from the experience. Without making excuses, we say, "This is something that I'm a part of, and I am 100 percent committed to take care of everything I can on my end." We concentrate on what we can improve and leave off assigning culpability.

5. **We avoid excuses.** A common way to shirk responsibility is to find an array of excuses. We may say we want to be more student-centered, but there's just not enough time. The truth is we *make* the time for things we truly value. There are always countless reasons for not doing the hard things, but we cannot allow them to deter us from pursuing our goals.

6. **We stand up to detractors.** We cannot afford to let our profession be dismantled by naysayers, doubters, complainers, whiners, and malcontents. Too often, positive momentum is derailed by loud, self-serving, and sometimes powerful people. We cannot uplift our profession by allowing others to promote fabrications and denigrate our work. We need to answer them with calm, assertive, well-thought out, truthful responses. (You'll find more on toxic people in Chapter 6.)

7. **We stop being our own worst enemies.** We reframe from having detrimental conversations about our classrooms, our schools, our districts, and other educators in public. We must maintain a realistic optimism about our profession. Yes, there are problems, and yes, there are many of us doing our best to solve them. We represent our schools and education everywhere we go. People listen to what we say because they assume we know "the truth." We need to stand together, support one another, and make every effort to speak positively about education. Our collective optimism can be contagious.

We Are Stronger Together

We live in an amazingly connected world that allows educators easy access to each other and to each other's resources. We encourage you to share your great ideas through appropriate internet connections (blogs, listservs, tweets, Pinterest, Instagram, or remarkable future programs yet to be designed). We are enthusiastic supporters of teachers attending conferences, webinars, virtual PD, and online courses that deal with their grade groups or disciplines (both as presenters and as attendees). We believe it is extremely helpful for educators to join the professional organizations who provide us with journals, conferences, webinars, online support, and other valuable services.

We realize that as teachers we are a vast and varied group. We teach different disciplines and age groups. Teachers work in urban schools, international schools, rural schools, online schools, public schools, private schools, as homebound teachers, in detention facilities, and in more situations than we can list. We have diverse (and sometimes *multiple*) personalities, talents, and experience levels. Nevertheless, we are united in our common love for being a part of the greatest profession, and we are responsible for maintaining its noble purpose.

Do What You Can

Because teachers are so diverse and bring so many different areas of expertise with them, teaching together can present all sorts of opportunities to make things better for everyone. We don't always have to wait for a committee or seek a quorum. Sometimes, we can just own it and act.

How You Can Make a Positive Impact on Education Policy

In his article, "Teachers Can Positively Impact Education Policy, We Just Have to Use Our Teacher Voice," Carlisle (2022) offers the following suggestions:

- **Write an op-ed.** Many news organizations create space for opinion editorials or letters to the editor. If they are interested in publishing your piece, most news organizations will have an editor provide you with two to three rounds of edits. Op-eds from educators can be particularly valuable because of their ability to impact the public discourse around a particular issue in education. In addition, having a published piece allows many people without classroom experience to hear firsthand how an existing or proposed policy impacts students, teachers, and schools.

- **Invite an elected official to your classroom.** Most elected officials don't have teaching experience, even those elected to state and local school boards. Furthermore, many elected officials who visit schools use their experience as justification for how they vote on specific policies. By inviting a school board member or legislator to your classroom, they witness the conditions created by policies and can hear directly from students and teachers what their needs are. These visits have the potential to be transformative and can shrink the distance between decision-makers and classrooms.

  For example, when a Texas State Board of Education member visited my classroom this year, he witnessed a discussion of how the contributions of women and scientists of color are often erased from science classrooms. The board member later shared with my principal that he was "blown away" by what my students shared, and he would take what he learned back to the board with him.

- **Testify at a public hearing.** For almost any proposed policy, the government entity introducing the policy must provide an opportunity for public comment. While most public testimony is limited to two or three minutes, this is one of the most powerful tools for change. Elected officials always share stories from their constituents about the impact of a policy. Because elected officials remember stories, sharing your experience in the classroom can make a difference.

- **Apply to a teaching policy fellowship.** Because getting involved in policy-making can be so tricky to navigate, this often results in giving up before even getting started. However, teaching policy fellowships can potentially be the most impactful route for advocacy. Not only do these policy fellowships work around your schedule as an educator, happening typically during the summer or evenings, but they have the added benefit of working with an organization that specializes in getting teachers involved in policy-making.

Being professionally responsible doesn't have to be overly taxing. Something as simple as tagging leaders and legislators when we post positive tweets, create memes, or write blogs can heighten awareness and promote healthy discourse.

Teacher-to-Teacher Feedback

If teachers are to act responsively and cohesively, we think it helps to have them involved in all aspects of staff building—recruitment, selection, observations, coaching, and providing feedback. In some schools, teachers are involved in each of these phases, and in other schools, they are involved in none. Many schools rely on instructional coaches to do the observing, coaching, and giving feedback. We agree that instructional coaches can be beneficial, especially for novice teachers and any teacher who is struggling in significant areas (e.g., classroom management, organizational strategies, data interpretation, etc.). However, we envision a collaborative spirit whereby teachers seek advice from their peers and reciprocate by doing the same. This teacher-to-teacher feedback promotes responsibility and helps teachers *own* their role in not only improving themselves but also in helping others grow.

Teacher-to-teacher feedback can be a powerful tool for improving instruction as it builds a collaborative accountability among teachers. It can be used for starting dialogues between teachers and creating channels for them to keep conversations going. Teacher-to-teacher feedback is not the traditional evaluative supervision model whereby an administrator drops in on a classroom unannounced, completes a rubric assessing a myriad of general categories observed at that one sitting, and schedules a debrief for an unspecified time in the future that may be days or weeks after the observation.

The teacher-to-teacher model carries no evaluation nor judgmental features. In this model, teachers are allowed to choose their observer(s) as well as decide on which class and which particular facet of their teaching they'd like to receive feedback (e.g., questioning strategies, time allotment, student engagement, or even their interaction with a specific student). The entire focus is on *improving* instruction. It is less formal, more interactive, and generally far more helpful than the classic teacher evaluations.

In teacher-to-teacher feedback, the procedure is generally as follows: (a) A teacher decides on an area they'd like to improve; (b) the teacher talks to a peer(s) about what kind of information they are seeking and sets up the time they'd like the peer(s) to visit; (c) the peer(s) drops in at the requested time, watches, listens, takes notes, and leaves; (d) As soon as possible, the teacher meets with the peer(s) for a debrief to share thoughts, discuss strategies, and think about how to improve.

When teachers don't have frequent, well-organized opportunities to work alongside and learn from their colleagues, the school squanders the precious human resources that it has worked so hard to gather.

—Susan M. Johnson

Steps for Teacher-to-Teacher Feedback

1. Define the feedback you're looking for.

2. Share the work.

3. Open up to feedback.

4. Reflect.

What School Leaders Must Do to Support Teacher-to-Teacher Feedback

Teacher-to-teacher feedback is more successful with strong support from school leaders. It can also be used in conjunction with instructional coaches. Quality training and implementation are key to the success of this practice. Building and sustaining a trusting community is a must. The logistics of making time for these observations and meetings can be challenging, and there is no one right way to do it. A School Retool (2022) offers suggestions. We paraphrased and added our own thoughts to the mix:

- Give teachers opportunities to observe each other. One day a week (or every two weeks or once a month), have open-door classrooms.

- Provide teachers a place to meet and give them protocol prompts to facilitate feedback (e.g., "What most impressed me was . . ." "Have you thought about . . ." "Tell me more about . . .").

- Dedicate the first ten minutes (or fifteen or twenty min.) of every staff meeting to teachers-teaching-teachers time.

- Give teachers a block of time to meet. Carve it out of PD time or build it into the regular schedule.

- Develop and foster school-wide community through joint work on a certain aspect of instruction starting with a focus chosen by the teachers.

- Link teachers with one another to facilitate communication and knowledge exchanges. Have your technology people create a private space for teachers to share informational feedback.

If we provide educators more opportunities to offer constructive feedback to each other, imagine all the knowledge we could unlock and share. Think of the growth and collaborative spirit we could ignite. The practice of giving and receiving productive feedback can help us elevate our skills and our competence. It can also help us to take ownership of our profession.

Action Step 4.3

MAKING PROFESSIONAL DEVELOPMENT COLLABORATIVE

The 5-minute video, *Teacher Labs: Making Professional Development Collaborative* demonstrates another kind of teacher-to-teacher feedback done in groups. Scan QR Code 4.3 to watch it and then ask yourself if this is something you would like to have in your school.

Active Listening

Most educators already know the key to better feedback is to employ the *active listening* skills we learned in every communications class we ever attended:

- Listen to understand

- Ask deeper questions

- Avoid interruptions

- Take nonverbal clues

- Slow down; practice silence

- Train your mind not to be distracted

- Withhold judgement

(Continued)

(Continued)

Jack Berckemeyer has added an interesting twist to active listening skills. He says at the beginning of a conversation, we should establish a purpose. We need to ask the speaker these three questions:

1. Do you want me to listen to what you're about to tell me so I can understand your point of view? **(Listen)**

2. Do you want me to listen so that I might give an opinion or advice? **(Respond)**

3. Do you want me to listen because you want me to take action to solve the problem? **(Solve)**

The answers to these questions set the stage to make us better listeners.

Sometimes, people just want to vent or speak out loud about something bothering them, but they aren't looking for and don't appreciate our opinions or advice. If they ask for our opinion or advice, they are not necessarily wanting us to do something about the situation. But sometimes what they really want is for us to use our position or authority to make something happen, and if so, we need to know that at the outset.

Giving Better Feedback to Our Peers

Planned observational feedback is not the only time we find ourselves needing to address an issue or a dilemma with a coworker. There are times we know we should speak up, but we remain silent because we don't want the other person to dislike us. We must remember that we can't control whether other people like us or not, but we can control how true we are to ourselves.

Sometimes, the hardest thing about giving feedback to our peers is our tendency to want to spare their short-term feelings, so we don't tell them the things they need to know about themselves. This *damaging empathy* is harmful because, by withholding valuable information, we rob them of a chance to become more competent. The ability to give and receive appropriate feedback is key to the success of teacher interactions and professional growth. Giving each other honest, carefully thought-out feedback creates deeper, more fulfilling relationships.

THE SECRET TO GIVING GREAT FEEDBACK

Scan QR Code 4.4 to watch the 5-minute video, *The Secret to Giving Great Feedback* and think about how you currently give feedback to peers. Is there something in this video you would like to try? What and Why?

> *We need to invite the elephant in the room in for tea.*
>
> —Cort (2022)

In their article, *12 Tips for Constructive Criticism and Peer Feedback*, Justworks (2020) lays out twelve areas for company peers to employ in giving feedback. We have trimmed theirs to eight and paraphrased them for our purpose of providing effective peer feedback in education.

Eight Tips for Constructive Feedback Among Educators

1. **Prepare.** Before you say the first word about the problem, think about what you are hoping to achieve with your conversation. Plan the best time and place to bring it up. Think about what words you want to use and which kinds of things you do NOT want to say (e.g., I need to let my neighbor teacher know that her voice is so loud and nasally that neither I nor my students can concentrate in our classroom. I should have the conversation in private and maybe even over drinks at Happy Hour. I don't want to tell her she sounds like Janice on "Friends." I do want to let her know the walls are thin, and some voices seem to carry more than others. I hope I can get her to lower her voice without hurting her feelings. But mainly I want her to lower her voice—especially that laugh.).

2. **Avoid the "feedback sandwich."** Most of us have been instructed to sandwich a critique between two compliments to soften a possible negative reaction. When a colleague senses what you're doing, it often backfires because it makes your compliments seem insincere and contrived, thus creating a mistrust from the beginning. If the colleague does

(Continued)

(Continued)

not know the sandwich ploy, they may get so caught up in the positive affirmations they don't even hear the feedback you sandwiched in the middle (e.g. "Fran, you have such an enthusiastic way about you. I just love your energy. Sometimes we can hear everything you are saying through the wall, and it disrupts my class, but hey, you've got a lovely spirit, and I wish I could be more like you.")

3. **Do it early, but don't catch them off guard.** The earlier you address the problem with a peer, the easier it is to fix the issue. Solving the problem early on will save you both time and energy. But don't catch them off guard. No one likes to be blindsided with bad news. Let them know you need to speak with them on an issue, or better yet, ask them for a good time for you to speak with them on an issue (e.g., It's probably not a good idea to bring up a tricky topic when a colleague is trying to get to class, rushing off to a doctor's appointment, or while you're both using the restroom.).

4. **Don't attack or insult.** This should be a no-brainer for those of us involved in the "people business," but as we have discussed throughout this book, it is better to be positive. The goal is to find solutions and not to be offensive. Just a simple statement of fact is better than emotion or sarcasm (e.g., Rather than fuming, "Pat, your constant frivolous disregard of school policies is unprofessional and frankly, a slap in the face to the rest of us. I am sick and tired of you undermining what us conscientious teachers are trying to do," say, "Pat, when you tell the students that our school dress code is a sham, it makes it harder for the rest of us to enforce the rules."). Of course, you will want to wait until you can speak in a calm, non-accusatory manner before you address a problem with a peer.

5. **Be clear and specific.** Using blur phrases like "kind of" and "it could be perceived as" or other expressions intended to avoid what the problem is will only make it worse. Say what you mean and be specific. We all know that words like "always," "never," and "usually," are ineffective when addressing a problem (e.g., Instead of, "Well, it can be kind of aggravating when you always spend more than your share of time using the copier—in some people's opinion, you—uh, sort of—their words, not mine—are usually hogging it when others need it, too," say, "You spent the entire lunch period using the team copier, and several of us also needed to use it. Can you help think of a way to make sharing it more equitable for all of us?").

6. **Use the passive voice.** Yes, we know English teachers have told us for years it is an ineffective way to write, but passive voice in feedback can be helpful in drawing the criticism away from the recipient while still focusing on the problem (e.g., Start with, "The interaction with your student earlier today was not the best" instead of "You were totally out of line with the way you embarrassed that poor kid in the hall."). Keep the focus on improving the work not putting the other person on the defensive.

7. **Make it a two-way conversation.** Listen to what your colleague has to say. Ask questions. Encourage the other person to think of alternatives and suggest their own solutions.

Adults do not like to be talked to like they are children (e.g. Instead of using a lot of "I woulds" or "You shoulds," state what you observed and ask for their take on things. Ask them, "Would you like to hear a different perspective?" rather than just presuming they are ready to receive your advice.).

8. **Put yourself in their shoes.** When planning to give constructive feedback, it helps to think about how you will be perceived. Think about how you would react and consider the information you know about a person's particular mind style (see Chapter 1). You want to be empathetic but not to the point it interferes with the purpose—improving the work. It is important that each educator hones their skills for giving constructive feedback. One way to get better at it is to focus on *receiving* critical feedback. Being able to share and to receive constructive feedback is crucial to owning a part in this profession.

Alex Kajitani, 2009 California teacher of the year, points out that while the success of the individual classroom rests on the relationship between the teacher and the students, the success of the entire school lies on the relationships among the adults in the building. He says, "Conflicts happen when human beings work together. How we deal with those conflicts is where we have the power to truly shape our school's culture" (Kajitani, 2016). We are each responsible for choosing optimism as the path we want for our schools.

●●● DISCUSSION QUESTIONS AND ACTION STEPS

1. In the scenario "Bad Teaching Day," what probably would have happened at your school after Dennis made his opening statement? What do you think is the best way to deal with a comment like Dennis made? Why?

2. Do you think it is hard to be honest with your colleagues about their choices and their actions? Why or why not?

3. What is your preferred method of receiving feedback? Why? What is your least preferred method of receiving feedback. Why?

4. What are (could be) some of the challenges of teacher-to-teacher feedback at your school? Are these things that can be overcome? Why or why not?

(Continued)

(Continued)

5. What is your opinion about teachers "policing their own ranks?" What does that phrase mean to you? Do you think if teachers did a better job of holding each other accountable, public opinion of teachers would improve? Why or why not?

6. When teachers are in public, should they refrain from making negative comments about the students, their colleagues, their leaders, or others involved with their schools? Is part of "owning it" defending our profession and our schools? If so, to what extent?

7. What is the best feedback you ever received on something to do with your teaching? What made it meaningful to you?

8. What is the worst type of feedback you ever received on something to do with your teaching? How did it impact you?

Action Steps for School Leaders

1. Fight for time for teachers to meet informally, reflect, and grow professionally. Encourage teachers to select their own areas for growth and assist them in getting the appropriate professional development opportunities they need.

2. Provide a classroom swap day where every staff member has to take the place of another staff member. Try to put people in jobs as far removed from their "normal jobs" as possible. End the day with a group round-up, and ask participants to share what they learned. Design funny questions for them to randomly answer about their day in the different job. This kind of activity is great for helping people understand the challenges others face.

3. Provide opportunities for teachers to visit each other's classrooms on a regular basis. Set up a schedule so that they can observe other teachers (individually or as a group) and then provide feedback and/or ask questions of the teacher. Some schools do this in a similar way to interns "making rounds" to learn from other doctors.

4. Provide opportunities for small groups of teachers to visit other school campuses. In a faculty meeting, have them share pictures and describe what they observed and learned.

5. Encourage teachers to select and attend conferences and other professional development activities that appeal to their interests. Whenever possible, put together a group of teachers who want to go to the same event, and you go with them. Attend sessions with them, dine

with them, and travel with them. Learn right along with them so that you can support them as they try new strategies and tools in their classrooms.

6. Set up a designated research area for teachers. Stock it with professional journals, books, and a computer that has connections to subscription services (e.g., Eric) for downloading journal articles.

7. Maintain a cloud-based inventory of onsite resources and materials for easy teacher access. Often teachers have no idea about what resources are available either because they are stored in an unorganized manner or some colleague has checked out certain materials to hoard in their classroom all year.

8. Reread the section, "What School Leaders Must Do" in this chapter and reflect on how you can best support teachers in their attempts to own their part in the profession.

MENTAL HEALTH *IS* HEALTH

Anything that's human is mentionable, and anything that is mentionable can be more manageable. When we can talk about our feelings, they become less overwhelming, less upsetting, and less scary.

—Fred Rogers

In her book, *Healthy Teachers, Happy Classrooms*, Tate (2022) points out that it is easier to think negatively than positively because our brains are biologically wired to breed negativity. The survival mechanism in early humans rewarded hunters and gathers for being acutely aware of threat and remaining hypervigilant in their daily activities. The unfortunate carry-over from our evolutionary history is a predilection toward pessimism. Tate emphasizes that optimism can impact stress levels and overall health.

Sometimes teachers tell us, "I just need to get rid of all the stress in my life." That is probably not a good idea. If you have absolutely no stress in your life, you are more than likely . . . um . . . dead. Our lives are an array of situations that demand a response to change. Some of the stress in our lives acts in a positive way to push us further, to give us energy, to help us anticipate new events. Weddings, births, vacations, graduations, and holidays cause us stress but, usually, in a good way. According to The American Institute of Stress, the term "stress," as it is currently used, was coined by Hans Selye, who in 1936 defined it as "the non-specific response of the body to any demand for change." Later, Selye realized that his term was being used synonymously with negative connotations, and he attempted to clarify that stress can be a positive force.

Preparing to meet a class on their first day of the school year, interviewing for a new assignment, hoping that a student will finally reach a much-anticipated milestone, and praying for pizza in the lunchroom rather than canned meat product are all examples of an excited tension that is not necessarily bad. Our days are filled with small and large occurrences that cause us stress. Most of these situations are not detrimental to our health. However, too many changes at once, major objectionable events, catastrophic disasters, unrelenting innocuous disturbances, and/or any combination of these can cause stress that undermines our physical well-being, our mental health, our personal relationships, our optimism, and our joy.

Self-Care Includes Our Mental Health

One of the reasons many teachers resent the sudden lip service to educator self-care is that most of the proposed measures don't solve the underlying structural problems in our schools. Educators point out that we cannot exercise or hydrate our way out of terrible class sizes, increasing behavioral problems, students facing or recovering from trauma, or the added pressure to get those test scores back up. Often, when asked about what could help with their well-being, teachers say, "Just give us additional time to plan and catch up, reduce our class sizes, limit our required number of meetings, and give us waivers on unrealistic academic expectations as we try to regain our balance." Granted, those are all parts of the educational infrastructure that need to be addressed, but in the meantime, is it not beneficial to work on the things we can control right now, like starting with our own bodies?

Chapter 3 offers several positive ideas for being proactive in meeting some of our bodies' overall health needs, but now more than ever, we need to address mental health (both for students and the adults who work with them). We give mental health its own chapter in this book because that's how important we think it is. Without good mental health, the other steps toward strengthening well-being are meaningless. Mental health *is* health.

Action Step 5.1

ASSESS YOUR DEPRESSION, ANXIETY, AND STRESS

Scan QR Code 5.1 to take this online test to compare your depression, anxiety, and stress levels with others. Look at your results and see if there are areas of mental wellness you need to work on.

On the test you took, were your levels of stress high? Hyper levels of stress can lead to depression and anxiety. Toxic stress can devastate our self-efficacy, our interpersonal relationships, our feeling of well-being, and our optimism. Ongoing negative stress has amplified for most educators in recent years, and it is something that needs to be dealt with. Rising stress levels are the body's response to lasting and serious worry in the absence of support to help us cope. Sound familiar?

At least the awareness of mental health and the need for treatment has also been growing in recent years. This is in large part due to campaigns designed to raise awareness about depression, addiction, anxiety, and toxic stress. Celebrities are starting to open up about their own mental health struggles, and that has helped bring attention to the problem. Despite this progress, many people who need help for a mental health issue won't seek it. There are several reasons why mental health has been ignored. The first reason is the associated stigma. The second is a perception of mental health disorders as "luxury indulgences" rather than actual illnesses. The third is limited access and inadequate funds.

Centralized Support for Mental Wellness of Staff Members

According to educational researcher Lee (2022), it's not a matter of *if* educators will experience the corrosive effects of prolonged and extreme stress but rather *when*. She strongly recommends that support is needed for more than just the students:

> Many school communities have focused on how teachers and administrators need to address the traumatic experiences students had during the pandemic, and not the impact of ongoing direct of vicarious trauma experienced by educators. To move toward healing and better supporting everyone, the effects of the pandemic on adults in learning communities need to be considered and addressed.

Lee's research team asked educators what might help them feel more supported by the schools. Three broad themes emerged:

1. Schools can play an active role in reducing stigma and barriers to mental healthcare, such as helping with accessing providers, removing financial obstacles, and offering dedicated, timely service for educators.

2. Schools can provide educators with safe space to consistently discuss experiences with fellow educators.

3. Schools can establish and maintain a culture of healthy work boundaries and relationships. (Lee, 2022)

By having a professional on site for teachers and other adults working in the building, schools can solve the problem of adults trying to schedule appointments after school during busy therapy provider times, reduce teacher travel time to and from therapy, and solve the waiting period of two or three months to see a provider. Schools can also reduce the excessive and often confusing paperwork for mental health insurance claims as well as set a standard for overcoming the social stigmas related to mental health.

Some schools and districts have already begun to address the problem of mental wellness directly:

> Knowing how taxing and upsetting the pandemic has been and that teachers have lost loved ones, El Rancho Unified School District in Pico Rivera, CA, developed an independent contract with a local licensed therapist this summer. Any staff member can contact her for therapy, counseling, or help in finding their own therapist for ongoing services through their insurance. (Najarro, 2021)

Schools can provide time and space for anxiety-ridden adults to begin to heal from the isolating impact of grief and trauma through the time-honored process of engaging with others in a place that fosters safe connection and supportive community. Teachers who have been allowed to meet in groups like this report how comforting it is to hear they are not alone and are encouraged by listening to how others have gotten through their struggles.

With the rapidly changing regulations and job demands, teachers and administrators together need to redefine setting boundaries. The pandemic and virtual teaching have added a new challenge. More parents are expecting on-demand feedback from teachers at times outside normal working hours. The boundaries between work and home have become blurred and sometimes overwhelming. Together, teachers and leaders need to agree on reasonable contact hours and operate together to reinforce them.

Modeling and Demonstrating Concern for Mental Health

Denver Schools' public health director, David Shapiro, talks about a program he wants to see in his schools:

For example, all school employees should learn how to access available supports for their own mental health needs. And schools should establish peer-support programs, so some employees learn, how to be an ally or "askable" adult for their colleague to get the support they need.

Shapiro recommends that districts train certain teachers or other staff members so there are "champions for mental health within the school district" who aren't in leadership positions. "After all, it can be intimidating to confide in your boss," Shapiro noted (Will & Superville, 2022).

A school in Louisiana began offering teachers the option to participate in individual therapy sessions with school social workers every other week. They later hired contract social workers in case teachers felt more comfortable talking with someone who wasn't on staff. The social workers kept all the information shared during the sessions confidential but also compiled top-level trends and shared that data with administrators.

Along with teachers, school leaders are feeling the weight of relentless stress. Ron Nozoe, the chief executive officer of the National Association of Secondary School Principals, has advocated for districts and schools to use some of their federal COVID-19 relief funds to set up targeted support programs for school leaders' mental health.

Action Step 5.2

HOW STRESS AFFECTS YOUR BODY

Scan QR Code 5.2 to watch the 4-minute video *How Stress Affects Your Body*. Make a list of things going on in your body right now that might be attributable to stress.

What Can You Do on Your Own to Reduce Unwanted Stress?

As with other aspects of our health, we can't control everything that goes on in our heads, but we can control the preventative health measures we take. It is imperative that we learn to mitigate stress factors with intentional steps toward more balance in our lives. Following the Four Principles of Deliberate Optimism, teachers must be aware of their personal needs, learn which factors affecting their health they can control, do the things that positively impact their welfare, and take responsibility for insuring their own well-being. See Appendix 5.1 for additional ideas for reducing stress.

If You Need Help, See an Expert

Educators are some of the worst procrastinators when it comes to seeking help for mental distress. Maybe it's because we've all taken classes in psychology or human behavior and consider ourselves experts in the field. Or maybe it's because we're so busy helping everybody else with their problems that we feel there's no time to concentrate on our own. Or perhaps we've just bought into that *Superman/Wonder Woman Teacher* image that makes us think we just need to *tough things out.*

Whatever the reason, it is absurd to think we can solve our own mental anguish by ourselves. Just as we counsel others to get help from experts, so should we. When we are clinically depressed, emotionally frazzled, or dealing with serious issues, it is important to remember that our friends and family may want to help us, but they can't. We need an unbiased third party to give us perspective and to listen without judgment. It is essential to seek out a counselor, cleric, psychologist, psychiatrist, or other trained mental health professional. Some even offer fees on a sliding scale, so cost doesn't have to be an issue.

Most of us have times in our lives when we need to hear the viewpoint of someone trained to deal with mental pain. Don't say to yourself, "This is ridiculous. I know a lot about mental health, and knowing what I know, I should be able to take care of this by myself." Instead, please say, "I am going through a tough time right now, and I could use the help of someone trained to deal with this kind of situation. This is the best investment of my time and money I can make right now. I am going to do this because I am worth it." Then do it. Sometimes the greatest demonstration of optimism is being able to reach out when you need help.

Managing Unwanted Stress

The first part to managing unwanted stress is to be aware of our stressors as well as our body's reaction to them. Because traditional work stress inventories ask things like "Do you try to do more than one thing at a time?" and "Are there a lot of deadlines in your work?" we find most of them useless for teachers. (Their stress indicators read like our job descriptions.) Therefore, Debbie put together the following stress indicators for educators.

Ten Ways You Know You Are An Educator Under Too Much Stress

Debbie Silver

1. You take two aspirin with your coffee every morning . . . just in case.

2. On the first day of school, you proclaim, "One down, 179 to go."

3. You go "street-rat crazy" on the person who parked in *your* parking spot.

4. You have nightmares all night about school, and the next day, you write referrals on the students who misbehaved in your dream.

5. You chase strangers' children down the aisles at the grocery store yelling, "We don't run at Krogers!"

6. When confronted by irate parents, you introduce yourself as someone else and pretend you can't speak their language.

7. You endlessly pop Bubble Wrap because you can't afford therapy.

8. You slap a coworker and yell, "Mosquito!" when there really wasn't a mosquito.

9. You leave footprints on the students' backs when the bell rings at the end of the day.

10. You take the same packed briefcase, backpack, tote bag, plastic crate, or cardboard box full of stuff back and forth to school each day without ever *touching* the contents inside.

© Silver (2015), revised.

If you did not laugh or even smile at this satirical stress indicator, it might be a sign that you truly are under way too much stress. Loss of a sense of humor is an indicator that we are overwhelmed and drained. Humor is a staple when it comes to dealing with stress. You don't have to be a stand-up comedian or even be able to tell jokes in order to make humor work for you. You just have to be able to appreciate the irony in life as well as chuckle at some of the insanity we all face. If we can't laugh at our common human foibles, what hope is there for us? Yes, education is a serious business, but we mustn't confuse that with taking *ourselves* too seriously. Self-deprecating humor is both healing and humanizing. It helps to disarm anger in others and allows us to stop, take a breath, and move to the reasoning part of our brain. Laughter forces a few steps—much needed distance—between stimulus and response.

Most laughter does not come from jokes. It comes from spending time with our family, our friends, and our colleagues. Laughing together is one of the best ways to build our immune systems, relax your bodies, lift our spirits, and build relationships. Good-spirited inclusive humor in a school can make all the difference in the world in creating an optimistic environment. A sense of playfulness among the adults is great for adult attitudes and relationships as well as a delight to the kids who watch our every move. Just be aware that there is a big difference between humor that includes and humor that excludes.

Inclusive Versus Excluding Humor

LAUGHING WITH OTHERS	LAUGHING AT OTHERS
1. Going for the jocular vein.	1. Going for the jugular vein.
2. Based on caring and empathy.	2. Based on contempt and insensitivity.
3. Builds confidence.	3. Destroys confidence.
4. Involves people in the fun.	4. Excludes some people.
5. A person enjoys being the "butt" of the joke.	5. A person does not have a choice in being made the "butt" of the joke.
6. Amusing, invites people to laugh.	6. Abusing, offends people.
7. Supportive.	7. Sarcastic.
8. Brings people closer.	8. Divides people.
9. Leads to a positive repartee.	9. Leads to one-man-down-manship cycle.
10. Pokes fun at universal human foibles.	10. Reinforces stereotypes.
11. Nourishing.	11. Toxic.
12. Icebreaker.	12. Ice maker.

Source: Reprinted with permission from Dr. Joel Goodman, Director of The HUMOR Project, Inc., in Saratoga Springs, NY (www.HumorProject.com). Originally appeared in Goodman's *Laughing Matters* magazine.

Take a Breath—Literally!

In dealing with a distraught child or student, our common first response to them is, "It's okay, just take a breath." Little did some of us know how much biological truth there was in that advice. Unless you teach on a remote island somewhere with no access to the internet or the outside world (so you are probably not reading this), you are familiar with the concept of *mindfulness*. Many self-care programs for educators are teaching and reinforcing the principle of slowing down the mind, taking in additional oxygen, and moving from the emotional part (amygdala) to the thinking part of the brain (prefrontal cortex). This long-established practice has been named many things, but today we generally call it *mindfulness*.

The practice of mindfulness usually focuses on concentrating, breathing, and making conscious choices. The act of intentionally slowing our breathing and actively trying to clear our minds of indiscriminate thoughts has a short-term effect on self-regulation and a long-term impact on the neuroplasticity of the brain. It is way of learning to be fully present in the moment without being distracted by past anxiety or future uncertainties. Mindfulness is a way to calm the emotional center of the brain through nonjudgmental and nonreactive awareness.

Action Step 5.3

WHY MINDFULNESS IS A SUPERPOWER

Scan QR Code 5.3 to watch the 2-minute video, *Why Mindfulness Is a Superpower.* Then reflect on how learning about and practicing mindfulness could benefit your mental wellness.

The straightforward act of pausing to connect with one's thoughts in a focused, nonjudgmental setting can yield remarkable feelings of awareness and control. Simply being able to label feelings and realize one has a conscious choice about whether or not to act on those feelings is empowering. For those new to this idea, we recommend that you speak with someone who already regularly practices mindfulness. There are numerous websites, podcasts, and other tutorials about how to do it. An easy way to start comes from the book, *Teaching Kids to Thrive: Essential Skills for Success* (Silver & Stafford, 2017).

The Five-Minute Mini-Meditation

Relax in the classroom, in your home, or just about anywhere with this five-minute mindfulness exercise.

1. Find a quiet spot to sit, lie, or stand. Pick a place where you won't be disturbed.
2. Get in a comfortable position.
3. Rest your hands on your legs or at your sides.
4. Either close your eyes or focus on a single point in front of you.
5. Listen to your breath as you inhale and exhale.
6. Try to focus on your breathing and not what is causing you stress or pain.
7. Breathe in slowly and exhale slowly. That is one count.
8. Continue until you complete about ten counts of breathing.
9. If your mind wanders and you lose count, start again.
10. Open your eyes or shift your focus.
11. Notice how you feel.
12. Were you able to calm yourself even a little?

—Silver & Stafford, 2017

Action Step 5.4

DECLUTTER THE MIND APP

If you love apps, a good one to download is *Declutter the Mind*. This could get you started in your practice of mindfulness. Scan QR Code 5.4 to learn more about the app at declutterthemind.com.

Mindfulness means paying attention in a particular way;
on purpose, in the present moment, and non-judgmentally.

—Jon Kabat-Zinn, 2017

Other Ways to Foster Mental Health

Probably we could write an entire book just on the topic of taking care of ourselves as teachers. Not only do we need to be at our personal bests for ourselves, but we are also role models for young people and often an inspiration to folks we don't even know about. Everyone knows the basics—eat right, get plenty of rest, exercise, and drink enough water. We have just a few more we would like you to consider because we think you are worth it. For a summary of how to deal with stress, see Appendix 5.1.

1. **Make sure you have a "go-to" person.** In Chapter 7, we discuss the importance of building relationships with colleagues. Hopefully there is someone at your school who is your *safety net*, someone who will stand by you no matter what. If you don't have that person at your school, try to cultivate a friendship with someone within at least an hour's drive from you who would come and help you no matter the time of day or night you called. How do you find somebody like that? As your mother always told you, "The best way to have that kind of friend is to be that kind of friend."

Definition of a Friend

A real friend will come and help you if you call no matter what the time of day or night.

A better friend will come and help you move.

A "go-to" friend will come and help you move bodies—no questions asked.

2. **Try to relax during some part of each day.** We are not recommending that you have Sven, the masseuse, pop in to give you a back massage during your unruly sixth-hour class or that you put on sunglasses, prop your feet on a table, and sing along with the Beach Boys' "Kokomo" playing on your iPod during a faculty meeting, but we do think it's imperative at least one time a day that educators find some way to break the tension of the rigorous work we do. Whether it is closing and locking your door, hiding out in the bookstacks in the media center, or even just sitting in your car in the parking lot, it is important to find some alone time to decompress and breathe, especially since teachers are almost never alone ("Yes, Tiffany René, I'll look over your report in just a minute—now please close my bathroom stall door and wait for me in the hall."). You can also read something inspirational, listen to soothing music, write in your journal, or just sit quietly and gather your thoughts.

> *Sacrificing your personal life to the classroom may seem like a sign of dedication, but is more likely to lead to burnout and bad attitude. We all need time to go home, turn the teaching dial down, and go back to being a person with a first name.*
>
> —Roxanna Elden, author of
> *See Me After Class* (as cited in Ferlazzo, 2013)

3. **Learn how and when to say "no."** We can't control everything that's going to happen, but we can control how we strengthen ourselves to handle the unknown. How many of you educators are presently thinking, "I just don't have quite enough things to do in my life. I'm a little bored. How can I get my superiors to add one or two more things to my plate?" That would be—no one! As a matter of fact, we believe that it should be a rule that no one can add another task to a teacher's assignments without removing something equally time consuming. One way to curb the temptation to multitask is to reduce the load we already have—or at least not add anything else.

Given that our time is already over committed and we are stretched as thin as we can stretch, many of us still lack the ability to say "no" when asked to handle even more responsibilities. Maybe because we see ourselves as helpers and caregivers, we feel compelled to step up and chair the math-a-thon, edit the student newsletter, sponsor the pep squad, donate a tutoring session, and dozens of other worthy causes that present themselves each year. Many times, we do it because it seems that no one else will do it and we can't live with the guilt of not volunteering.

We (the authors) are all for volunteering. We think being willing to help others is part of our noble profession, and individuals ought to give their time, talent, and material assets to others when they choose to. The problem comes when we commit to more things than we can effectively do. It is so easy to say, "Yes, I'll help with that," when the task is six months away (Always remember: Dates are closer than they appear on the calendar!). Then when the time is upon us, we lament, "Oh, I can't believe I let them talk me into doing this. I don't even have time to dust my plant leaves, let alone take care of this chore!" Seriously, we think teachers should carefully select the causes they most want to support and leave the rest to others. When we over-commit, we become "non-joyful givers," and that defeats the whole purpose of giving, right? It also adds to our stress levels.

Have you ever noticed that no matter what the request made of faculty members, there are always one or two who never get pressured into volunteering nor seem to feel guilty about not stepping up? Do you secretly envy their ability to say "no" and get away with it? Do you sometimes wish you could be a little more assertive about not getting roped into things you wish you had not agreed to do? Perhaps it is time you learned the secret to avoiding being manipulated into over-committing.

First, stop volunteering for things you cannot do, do not wish to do, or do not have the time or energy for. If you are asked directly to take on another responsibility, you need to think about your personal well-being and the effect the added responsibility will take on your time and stress level. The art of saying "no" to a colleague or to an administrator begins with a little assertiveness training. You do not need to be aggressive, hostile, or rude, but you do need to mean what you say. Don't whine, hedge, or offer an apology.

Scenario: In a faculty meeting, the administrator is trying to enlist volunteers for a special project. He spies you and beguilingly pleads, "Theresa, I really need a sponsor for this year's Help-A-Child Foundation, and you are such a terrific organizer, I'd like to enlist your help. As you know, this event is an important part of our community's outreach to needy children, and of course, being a parent yourself, I know you'll want to contribute. Just look at these pictures I have of young children with sad little smudged faces. Doesn't it just break your heart? May I count on you to take over this year's fundraiser?"

Normal responses are, "I'd like to help, but I don't have time." "Oh gee, I can't do it at this time." "Well, I'd like to help but. . . ." None of these are what an assertive person says because they leave you open for arguments and more appeals. Don't allow any discussion on the issue, and don't say, "I can't do it this time" because it sounds like you are volunteering for next year. In her workshops on teacher time management, Debbie Silver suggests that individuals give a three-point response.

Three-Point Response

In a calm but firm voice you say the following:

1. "I appreciate the vote of confidence." (In other words, stop blowing smoke up my dress; you're not going to flatter me into this.)

2. "I think the Help-a-Child Foundation is a worthy cause, and I hope this year's event is a tremendous success." (So quit showing me pictures of sad little kids, trying to manipulate me with sob stories, or otherwise selling me on the cause. I'm sure it's a great cause, but that's not the point.)

(Continued)

(Continued)

3. "For several reasons, I have to say, 'No.'" (Then break eye contact—he who blinks, loses. Do not hedge, mumble, or whine. Clearly and succinctly turn down the offer, and shift your attention to other things—or better yet, walk away. Assertive people state their cases simply and quietly and offer no explanation or apology.)

Most importantly, don't feel guilty or responsible. By not volunteering for everything that comes your way, you can often nudge others into roles they may need to try. You also save your time and attention for causes that are personally gratifying to you and, therefore, cause you less stress. Being a *non-joyful giver* does not help you or the cause in the long run. Say "no" and mean it.

Practice the three-point response until you can do it without an apologetic voice, any additional explanation or lingering guilt. Your time is one of your most precious commodities. Take control of it and invest it carefully.

© Silver (2015)

4. **Pay attention to your life outside your job.** It seems simplistic to state that in order to take care of others, educators must first take care of themselves, but many in our field make truly unhealthy choices in our own lives as we skip meals, forego sleep, work incredibly long hours nightly and on weekends, and generally put every ounce of energy we have into our jobs. There need to be a balance. Maybe it's time to stop wearing teacher overtime as a badge of honor. Maybe part of our burn-out problem comes from the belief that overwork is the mark of a good teacher.

A former state teacher of the year tells us that she was relentless in doing her job as a teacher. She committed to working for her students day and night and was very proud of how she was able to rear her own three sons and still do all the extras it took to be an outstanding educator. Years later when having a discussion with her grown-up sons, she told them she was surprised they were not more altruistic. Her oldest son replied, "Gee, Mom, I wonder why we're not." Seeing the confusion in her face, he continued, "Mom, did it ever occur to you that sometimes we just needed you to be *our* mom? Everywhere we went with you your students would hug you and tell you they wished you were their mom, or they'd want to sit with us, or they'd interrupt us so they could talk to you. At night when we wanted to tell you stuff, you were on the phone talking to your students' parents or grading papers or preparing things for your class the next day. You were a great teacher, but sometimes we needed you to be just our mom."

The increased amount of work that has come with the pandemic and its aftermath has many teachers struggling harder than ever to maintain the balance between school and work. Katy Farber believes that teachers' hypervigilance and stress fatigue can have negative impacts on our families:

> Teachers have dealt with every scenario at school—physically, emotionally, intellectually. That's why our loved ones sometimes see an empty stare at the end of the day. We teachers have used up all our energy for decisions, protection, care, safety, emotions at school. There is nothing left at the end of the day. No tolerance for big toddler tantrums, long conversations, negotiations with tweens and teenagers, making plans and logistics. We are often unable to respond to the needs of our families with active, compassionate listening, decision-making, or planning. (Farber, 2022)

Action Step 5.5

BEFORE YOU OPEN THE DOOR, SMILE

Scan QR Code 5.5 to watch Benjamin Holmgren's *Before You Open the Door, Smile* 2.5-minute video about a dad's Facebook post that went viral. Scroll down and click on the picture to read post itself. Ask yourself why it is important to shift your entire focus from work to your family when you get home.

There you have it. We've laid out positive, proactive things we educators need to do to take care of mental health. Simple steps, right? Most of you are nodding your heads and saying, "Yes, I know I need to work on. . . ." Whatever it is that goes in the next part of that sentence for you, please do it. Students are counting on you. Your family is counting on you. And you are so worth it!

●●● DISCUSSION QUESTIONS AND ACTION STEPS

1. Try your hand at writing your own Top Ten Ways You Know You Are an Educator Under Too Much Stress. Be as funny and as creative as you can. If you don't mind sharing, please forward your list (along with names and schools of the writers) to debbie@debbiesilver.com. We promise to mention you in any ideas we "borrow" for future publications.

(Continued)

(Continued)

2. Do you agree with Diana Lee's statement, "It's not a matter of *if* educators will experience the corrosive effects of prolonged and extreme stress, but rather *when*." Explain your answer.

3. Would you talk with a counselor if one were provided to you by your school or district? Why or why not?

4. We state in the book that people in mental pain should speak with an unbiased third party. Why might that be preferable to depending on friends and relatives for advice?

5. Name examples of inclusive humor you have used or witnessed. How did it affect the people involved? Name examples of exclusive humor you have been a part of or witnessed. How does exclusive humor affect a culture?

6. Does your school offer training in or practice any kind of mindfulness? Do you see any value in taking a moment to breathe slowly to clear your mind as a way of alleviating unwanted stress? Do you know people who regularly practice mindfulness? What do they have to say about it?

7. What person did you think of when you read about having a "go-to" friend? Take a moment to call, text, email, or go in person to tell them they were the first person who came to your mind. Tell them how grateful you are to have them in your life.

8. What are some things educators can do to maintain a sense of calm at school? What do you do?

9. How do educators find the right balance between school life and home life? Do you think you have found a reasonable balance? Why or why not?

10. When asked to "volunteer" for extra assignments and work you don't want to do, what is the benefit of using the Three-Point Response? How is that preferable to the answer, "I'm just too busy right now to take on another thing. Are you going to be mad at me if I say, 'no'?"

Action Steps for School Leaders

1. DeMatthews and Su-Keene (2022) state that a popular coping strategy for administrators is meeting with fellow principals for drinks, dinners, or informal check-ins. They say that principal support networks are critical to managing job-related stress. Do you regularly meet with this kind of support group? Why or why not? What could you do to start or reinvigorate this kind of group for you and your peers?

2. Employ good-spirited humor to encourage positive communication and to ease tense situations. Encourage staff members to do the same. Smiling and good-natured laughter are two indicators of a healthy school climate.

3. When you are aware that a teacher is having a particularly stressful time, volunteer to either assist with their class or take over their class while they do what they need to do to get themselves together. When they thank you, simply tell them, "It was my pleasure. You're worth it." And never mention it again.

4. Once a month, provide food for the adults at school as a special acknowledgement for their efforts. It can be as simple as bagels and juice for breakfast or as easy as a potato bar set up in the teacher lounge/workroom during lunch.

5. Provide free coffee, tea, and water in the teacher lounge or in a central location for staff throughout the day.

6. Use funny or inspirational video clips to begin faculty meetings.

   Never miss an opportunity to affirm the great things staff members do for the kids and for the school.

7. Stay tuned to the dynamics in your building. If the superintendent just gave a talk on how the school board is in the mood for budget slashes, it may be time for you to bolster morale via a teacher retreat or just hanging around the workroom offering reassurances.

8. Sit in the back of a classroom and imagine what it would be like to teach the students in that room. Make a list of the pluses and minuses on being a teacher on your campus. Think about what you are asking your teachers to do. Is it fair and reasonable? Would you be able to do what you are asking them to do?

"BUT WE HAVE THIS *ONE* TEACHER WHO KEEPS RUINING EVERYTHING!"

Don't try to win over the haters; you are not a jackass whisperer.

—Brown (2013)

It's Important in Our Business to "Work Well With Others"

When Jack Berckemeyer presents to teachers on team building, he often hears the comment, "I agree with most of what you are saying, but we have this *one* teacher who keeps ruining everything!" We've all heard some form of that complaint (e.g., "We wouldn't have these personnel problems if it weren't for that one person." "If we could just get rid of that guy, everything would be perfect." "I'm all about giving people a second chance, but I'm so done with her!").

When adults are asked what factors make their work rewarding, most include the people they work with. In surveys, a person's workplace colleagues are repeatedly valued over pay, vacation time, a bigger title, or even paid health insurance (SHRM, 2011).

Being attentive to the needs of one's students and developing new strategies for their success are demands that never diminish. And despite the many hours we spend with students, they are not our primary workplace colleagues; indeed, they are not *colleagues* at all. The teachers on our team, in our department, or at our grade level are. They are the ones who will offer support (or not), share our successes and failures (or not), bolster us when we are down (or not), and celebrate with us when things are going splendidly (maybe—if there's cake involved).

We have all wanted to tell some educators, "Honey, it's okay to have a bad day, maybe even a bad year, but you are having a bad career—do us all a favor and leave this profession now!" And perhaps in reaction to the few truly mean-spirited educators, that would seem the best solution. However, more often we find that the adults who have chosen to work every day with kids are people worth the extra effort it sometimes takes to bring them into a positive community relationship.

Our adult colleagues throughout the school help us accomplish our individual aims and the collective goals of the school. Forming positive relationships with the various collaborators in the building makes the workplace more enjoyable and gives us the energy we need to face the continuing pressures of being a teacher. We can't escape the fact that we all have a psychological need for affiliation. When a teacher is supported by professional adult relationships, their classroom work improves and their connections with students benefit. Team and faculty discussions are more fruitful when individuals are familiar with other members of the group. Good ideas are brought forward. Positive conflicts are more easily resolved. Because our workplace is where we spend most of our entire day and because real learning is nearly always based on relationships, making these connections is imperative.

It's challenging when some of the grown-ups with whom we relate are not exactly filled with joy. They complain, criticize, or manifest supreme apathy about their work as educators. How can we build relationships with colleagues who are constantly negative or who seem to want nothing more than to get through the day with as little effort as possible? Realistic optimists first try to reframe their perspectives on their teammates. They conscientiously gather many views about the other person's actions and motivations. They pay attention to mindstyle (Chapter 1) and consider as many variances as possible (e.g., generation, extrovert/introvert, gender, race, culture, socioeconomic status, experiential background, and other individualities) that sometimes divide us. Gathering as much information as we can about a colleague helps us build an empathy with that person, which according to researcher Brené Brown is the only way to build genuine bonds with others. She states, "I define connection as the energy that exists between people when they feel seen, heard, and valued; when they can give and receive without judgment; and when they derive sustenance and strength from the relationship" (Brown, 2010).

Generational Differences

For the first time in our history, we have four and sometimes even five different generations working in the same school. Social psychologists and other researchers point out that each generation comes with its own distinct attitudes, expectations, and habits regarding work. At times, we may find ourselves at cross-purposes merely because of when we were born. Although there is a difference of opinion on some of these ranges, generally the ranges fall in or close to the following periods.

GENERATIONAL TENDENCIES

Figure 6.1 provides an overall summary of generational differences. Of course, each of us wants to be cautious about "painting with too broad a brush." The purpose of exploring generational tendencies is to think about different perspectives aligned with something individuals can't change—when they were born. Rather than categorizing people by their age, we need to have an understanding that why they behave in certain ways has nothing to do with us and is all about their age group.

Figure 6.1

Generational Tendencies

Traditionalists

Born 1925–1945

Dependable, straightforward, tactful, loyal

Shaped by: The Great Depression, World War II, radio, and movies

Motivated by: Respect, recognition, providing long-term value to work

Communication style: Personal touch, handwritten notes instead of email

Worldview: Obedience over individualism; age equals seniority; advancing incrementally through the hierarchy

Baby Boomers

Born 1946–1964

Optimistic, competitive, workaholic, team-oriented

Shaped by: The Vietnam War, civil rights movement, Watergate

Motivated by: Organization loyalty, teamwork, duty

(Continued)

(Continued)

Communication style: Whatever is most efficient, including phone calls and face-to-face

Worldview: Achievement comes after paying one's dues; sacrifice for success

Generation X
Born 1965–1980

Flexible, informal, skeptical, independent

Shaped by: The AIDs epidemic, the fall of the Berlin Wall, the dot-com boom

Motivated by: Diversity, work-life balance, their personal-professional interests rather than the organization's interests.

Communication style: Whatever is most efficient, including phone calls and face-to-face

Worldview: Favoring diversity; quick to move on if their leader fails to meet their needs; resistant to change at work if it affects their personal lives

Millennials (sometimes called Generation Y)
Born 1981–2000

Competitive, civic-minded, open-minded on diversity, achievement-oriented

Shaped by: Columbine, 9/11, the internet

Motivated by: Responsibility, the quality of the leader, unique work experiences

Communication style: IMs, texts, email

Worldview: Seeking challenge, growth, and development: a fun work life and work-life balance; likely to leave an organization if they don't like changes

Generation Z
Born 2001–2020

Global, entrepreneurial, progressive, less focused

Shaped by: Life after 9/11, the Great Recession, access to technology from a young age

Motivated by: Diversity, personalization, individuality, creativity

Communication style: IMS, texts, social media

Worldview: Self-identifying as digital device addicts; valuing independence and individuality; preferring to work with millennial leaders, innovative coworkers, and new technologies

Adapted from Purdue University Global, n.d., https://www.purdueglobal.edu/education-partnerships/generational-workforce-differences-infographic/

Scenario: The Team Meeting

A multigenerational team of five teachers is gathered for a meeting. During a quick exchange of ideas, Traditional Terry asks people to slow down and repeat what they are saying so that he can write down their responses for the minutes. X'er Xandra sighs and asks him when he's going to join the twenty-first century and start using an iPad with a recording app.

Millie Millennial says, "OMG, are you seriously writing out every word we say? J2LYK nobody does that. XME but, Dude, that is seriously lame."

Zelda Z'er chimes in, "You guys need to be kinder to each other. I'm not feeling safe with your confrontational tones."

Terry glares at the three of them and continues to write. Benny Boomer interjects, "Okay, let's move on, shall we? We agreed that we need to challenge the district mandate, and we have this school board presentation to finish. I thought I'd take the lead on this and speak for our group."

Millie responds, "Since Zelda and I are the ones who made the final iMovie about it, wouldn't it make more sense for us to present it to the board?"

Benny chuckles, "Well, Mille, I hardly think you're ready to take the lead. I mean you're not really a veteran teacher, and I don't think people will take you seriously. Why don't you wait until you've been in the trenches a little longer before you start speaking up about something the rest of us have been dealing with since before you were born?"

Terry nods in agreement. "Besides that, Benny and I are the ones who did all the hard work on this project. Yesterday the three of you left early to go to your Lady Googa, or whatever she's called, concert and didn't stick around to help. We're the ones who've stayed here day after day working to ten some nights trying to hammer this thing out while you three had to have your *me time*."

Xandra rebuts, "Look, Millie, Zelda, and I work hard, too, you know. It's just that we know how to work a little smarter and not waste time doing things the old-fashioned way. I don't know what the big deal is anyway. The board is just a bunch of old fossils who only care about getting reelected."

Bennie argues, "Look, I'm sure the board members will change their minds once we show them how hard we have worked to create something that is better for our students. Also, I'm personal friends with a couple of them, so I think I'm the one who should make the presentation."

Terry adds, "And at least Benny won't go in there and offend people with an entitled attitude. In my day, young people showed a lot more respect for their elders."

Millie gathers her stuff, grabs Zelda's arm, exits, and says over her shoulder, "Well, it's not your day anymore, and all I can say is IMHO you can DIY."

Terry asks, "What did she say?"

Benny shakes his head and mutters, "I have no idea."

The Team Meeting scenario was written tongue-in-cheek to begin a workshop on generational differences. Gently poking fun at ourselves sometimes opens the doors for deeper examination of serious issues. But educators still need concrete actionable steps to help clear the hurdles of biases. Here are some examples of building trust among generations that can be modified for many different prejudgments that groups may need to address.

Six Ways to Build Trust Between Generations

1. **Reverse Mentoring**

   Whatever our role or our generation, we need to engage in a mentoring relationship and reverse mentoring to build long-lasting trust. Reverse mentoring allows different generations to mentor each other from their areas of strength. It is about learning and forming trust between generations.

2. **Roundtable Experiences**

   Many conference tables are rectangular. We choose sides. Someone sits at the head of the table. That sets an implied structure. We need to imagine a ROUND table where all voices have an equal say and important insights. We must drop our role and our organizational and generational stiffness. Free-flowing exchanges and open mindsets create trust between generations.

3. **Focus on Individual Uniqueness and Talents**

   Generalizations don't always apply and can be distracting from the talents, perspectives, and gifts someone can bring to the work to be done, the problems to be solved, or the initiatives to be achieved. Empathy helps develop trust between generations.

4. **Ask Questions to Learn**

   We need to do less talking to and more questioning of one another. Good questions lead to good conversations. Good questions coupled with undistracted listening leads to better trust between generations.

5. **Move Beyond the Headlines**

   Headlines often offer distortions and misinformation about generational tendencies. Digging deeper into the information raises our awareness and understanding. More importantly, skip the surveys and join a different generational group in conversation. It will be much more valuable and build trust in much better ways.

6. **Focus More on Character and Less on Characteristics**

   Character matters most. We need to move beyond the intense focus on characteristics and focus more on character. We need to mentor when we can, guide where we must, and develop a fruitful exchange of ideas and principles all the time. This is where trust takes root and grows.

Adapted from Mertz (2013)

Discussing Diversity

Action Step 6.1

CULTIVATING CALMNESS

Brené Brown speaks on how to have difficult conversations about race and other issues in *Cultivating Calmness*. Scan QR Code 6.1 to watch this 4-minute video. Do you agree with Brown's ideas about how to approach conflict? What would you add or change?

Speaking candidly about the things that divide us helps us to break down labels and work toward greater understanding of and empathy with each other. Whether addressing generational differences, issues of race and culture, political division, gender, sexual orientation, and so forth, the following rules can help set the tone for the desired outcome.

Diversity Workshop Ground Rules
Debbie Silver

- Personal information shared during this workshop remains confidential.

- No side conversations that exclude others.

- No talking over others.

- Disagree respectfully rather than with put-downs or judgmental criticism.

- Don't give feedback to others unless you are asked specifically to do so.

- Refrain from making generalizations or invoking stereotypes about groups.

- Feel free to speak up about issues important to you. Don't be afraid to ask questions, question answers, or bring up sensitive points.

- Feel free to stop and think rather than speak immediately. This workshop is designed to be reflective as well as instructive.

- Remember that today's topics often make people uncomfortable and building an inclusive community is an ongoing process.

Taking the time to consider the other person's perspective goes a long way toward bridging miscommunication gaps and beginning to form some sort of alliance with them. Before we "vote people off the island," we at least need to try to give them the benefit of the doubt. Deliberate optimists are those who try to see the best in others and believe that most people are doing the best they can.

> *When you finally learn that a person's behavior has more to do with their internal struggle than it ever did with you, you learn grace.*
>
> —Allison Aars

Extroverts and Introverts

When our first edition of *Deliberate Optimism* went out for reviews, one administrator criticized us for broaching the topic of introverts and extroverts. His comment was, "I don't understand the need to talk about introverts and extroverts in a book about teachers. Everyone knows that *all* teachers are extroverts." We love to share that comment with teachers and listen to them roar with laughter.

On every staff, there are those who seems to really dislike team-building games, "rah-rahs," and getting in a group to create a poster. Even when you try to include them in your group, they resist. They decline invitations to special faculty events, and sometimes, they seem to prefer eating alone in their rooms rather than joining others in the lounge or lunchroom. It would be easy to label them as aloof, unfriendly, cold, detached, or even unapproachable. We have heard teachers say about such a person, "Well, I guess she just thinks she's too good to hang out with the rest of us. Maybe we're not worthy of her attention." Those kinds of comments are generally made by someone who defines themselves by the friends they have and have little understanding of people who draw strength from being alone.

When you study personality theory, you inevitably come across the terms *introvert* and *extrovert*. We authors (Debbie and Jack) are generally classified as extroverts for most situations. As extrovert teachers, we tried to *fix* our introverted students so they could enjoy a more robust, fulfilled lifestyle. When dealing with colleagues, we felt sorry for the introverts and jumped in quickly to fill the gaps when they didn't speak, commit, or participate. On reflection, we see that we did not do them any favors.

Most of us were taught that introverts are simply people who are shy. Extroverts, on the other hand, are outspoken, confident, and filled with leadership potential. Recently, much has been written on the subject of introversion and how it has been misinterpreted. Behavior experts contend that introversion itself is not shyness. Shyness has an element of apprehension, nervousness, and anxiety, and while an introvert may be also shy, introversion itself is not shyness. Basically, an introvert is a person who is energized by being alone and whose energy is generally drained by being around other people (Cherry, 2022).

In her book, *Quiet: The Power of Introverts in a World That Won't Stop Talking*, journalist/researcher Cain (2012) points out that an introvert might identify with at least some of the following attributes: thoughtful, serious, inner-directed, calm, sensitive, unassuming, shy, and solitude seeking. Conversely, an extrovert might identify with some of these attributes: gregarious, excitable, active, risk-taking, light-hearted, and thick-skinned. While not comprehensive, this list serves as a starting point to understanding the differences between the two categories.

Cain states that nearly one third of the people we know are introverts. In an era that values outgoing, charismatic people who demonstrate confidence, a kind of *extrovert ideal* has marginalized that third, who sometimes are our deepest, most thoughtful thinkers. Perhaps in trying to understand our quieter colleagues, we need to rethink how we sometimes talk over them, ignore them, and otherwise dismiss them as not as important as their more forceful peers.

> The funny thing about introverts is once they feel comfortable with you, they can be the funniest, most enjoyable people to be around. It's like a secret they feel comfortable sharing with you. Except the secret is their personality.
>
> —Anonymous

One of the key informational pieces we need to understand about the people with whom we work (both our colleagues and our students) is whether they are predominantly introverts or extroverts. Most of us are knowledgeable about dealing with extroverts, but could an intentional focus on the introverts in our lives help us better understand how to interact with them? Rockwell (2013), author of the blog *Leadership Freak*, warns against underestimating quiet people. He cautions that it is dangerous to assume that silence is consent and urges colleagues to give quiet people a chance to collect their thoughts before they have to make a commitment or frame an answer.

In his blog post *10 Ways to "Deal With" Quiet People*, Rockwell (2013) advises the following:

1. Honor their strengths. Never say, "Oh, they're quiet," like it's a disease.

2. Respect their ability to commit. When they're in, they're in.

3. Give them prep time. Don't spring things on them.

4. Don't assume silence is disagreement or consent. Just don't assume.

5. Enjoy silence. Give them space by closing your mouth.

6. Ask questions, after you have given them think-time.

7. Invite feedback one-on-one rather than in groups.

8. Walk with them after meetings and ask, "What's going through your mind?" The walking part is important.

9. Create quiet environments. Quiet people often enjoy quiet places.

10. Let them work alone. Stop demanding group work.

If you are not an introvert, it is important to familiarize yourself with their characteristics and tendencies. Most of them enjoy being with a few trusted associates occasionally, but they thrive on *downtime* when they can spend moments alone rejuvenating themselves. If you are an introvert, you need to understand that extroverts like to *think out loud*, and try not to judge them harshly because of their excessive chatter. Extroverts are as energized by being around others as you are from spending time alone. Knowing all we can about one another's preferences is the first step toward building healthy communication among educators.

Action Step 6.2

6 STRUGGLES ONLY INTROVERTS COULD RELATE TO

The 2.5-minute video *6 Struggles Only Introverts Could Relate To* can validate your feelings if you are an introvert and inform you about others who are not like you if you are an extrovert. Scan QR Code 6.2 to watch it and see if you identify with it or can think of colleagues who do.

But Still, There's That
One Teacher . . .

Have you ever felt that it would be easier to be optimistic if you could just get rid of one or two (or 10 or 20) of your colleagues? Debbie Silver's comedy persona, a curmudgeon schoolteacher named Rhodeena Culsmucker, is the classic pessimist. She sees only the negative in her administrators, her students, and her colleagues. A sharp decrease in the joy factor is felt the moment she walks into a gathering. She is cynical, critical, mean-spirited, and of course, quite verbal. She is the antithesis of what we want and need from our colleagues. And yet, every time our author portrays her in a comedy skit, teachers immediately say, "Oh my gosh, I work with a guy (or gal) just like that!"

In truth, the character Rhodeena Culsmucker speaks to every teacher because she is the epitome of our very worst selves. We laugh at her because her growling and complaining echo our lowest thoughts and even things we have said in our own flawed moments. She's funny because she's not a real teacher. Actual negative strident colleagues are vexations to the soul. They are not funny, and they can be quite damaging not only to those around them but also to an entire school environment.

Gathering information and accepting people for who they are is quite different from actually liking or even respecting them. Working with toxic people can drain the optimism and the energy right out of a person. And true, there usually is that *one* teacher who really does ruin things for everyone (including school leaders, colleagues, and students). So what do we do about that person?

> You don't ever have to feel guilty about removing toxic people from your life. It doesn't matter whether someone is a relative, romantic interest, employer, childhood friend, or a new acquaintance—you don't have to make room for people who cause you pain or make you feel small. It's one thing if a person owns up to their behavior and makes an effort to change. But if a person disregards your feelings, ignores your boundaries, and "continues" to treat you in a harmful way, they need to go.
>
> —Danielle Koepke

Minimizing the Impact of Toxic People

Action Step 6.3

5 PIECES OF ADVICE FOR DEALING WITH TOXIC PEOPLE

Scan QR Code 6.3 to watch this 4-minute video *5 Pieces of Advice for Dealing With Toxic People,* from five famous speakers. Do you agree with what they offer? What would you add to their ideas?

Realistically, sometimes you may feel you have done all you can and the other person still saps your energy, your passion, and your delight in what you do. It may be time to move on to our Deliberate Optimism Principle #2: Control What You Can. None of us can change another person. Even with the best intentions, it is not possible to make someone love us, like us, or even respect us. How others feel about us is really none of our business. It's their choice. There are certainly things we can do to try and enhance relationships, but in the end, it is up to them to decide whether or not and to what degree they wish to participate in a positive relationship. Hopefully, we are self-assured enough to make several efforts to include everyone in our positive community, but occasionally, there is someone who just doesn't "play well with others." What do you do about that mean-spirited, antagonistic, negative colleague or administrator?

Once you have identified a person as someone within whose presence you feel small, unappreciated, targeted, or demeaned, the best gift you can give yourself is to put as much distance (physically and emotionally) as you can between him and you. We call it, "staying away from *talking snakes.*" We recommend that all adults treat each other with respect and professionalism at work, but beyond that, it is important to focus on controlling your interactions with negative people. We can't always choose the people with whom we work, but we can learn to identify the *talking snakes* and "cut them a wide path."

Avoiding *Talking Snakes*

1. Be polite but share minimal information about yourself, your class, or your achievements. Your success threatens them, and your failures delight them. Keep your conversations with them light and business oriented.

2. In social situations, do not willingly join a group they are already in or they frequently attend. If the negative person is "holding court" in the teacher's lounge, find somewhere else you need to be. Without drawing attention to what you are doing, always try to manipulate your way out of places where the talking snake is present.

3. If the negative person tries to bait you into an argument, take the high ground and use the Stephen Covey line, "I guess we will just have to agree to disagree on that point." Walk away.

4. Do NOT gossip. If you have a trusted friend, you can share your feelings about Mr. or Ms. Negative, but other than that, stay as neutral as you can whenever that person's name is mentioned. Never let students, parents, or casual acquaintances initiate defaming conversations or repeat derogatory information about the talking snakes. Such indulgences are not helpful and will only further drain your positivity.

5. Realize that everyone may not see the person the way you do. Don't force colleagues to take sides. Politely decline with a reasonable excuse any invitations that include the negative person and leave it at that. Let others make their own decisions about dealing with snakes.

6. There will be times when you cannot avoid the person (they may be on your team or teach next door to you). Figure out what you can control and do it. With a polite smile on your face, you can repeat this mantra in your mind, "I may be forced to work with you, but I am not required to like you. I will work with you for the benefit of our students, but you are getting none of the personal real estate I have in my head. I've got more positive things to think about."

7. We recommend that you try to diminish as much as possible the time you give yourself to think about the snakes in your life. In desperate situations, you might consider asking to be transferred to another grade group, wing, or even a different school. You can try to negotiate a different lunchtime and planning period from them. You can park your vehicle in a spot far removed from where the offending party parks and plan your arrival and departure times different from theirs.

8. Focus on your students, your team, and your personal goals. Don't waste energy worrying about what the *snakes* are doing. (Unless you believe they are doing harm to kids or bullying weaker teachers—then you have a moral obligation to speak up.) Time and energy focused on people who do not want to change is a waste. Try to stay focused on the people who value and appreciate you.

You're Not Being Paranoid if They Really *Are* After You! (Bullying in the Workplace)

Sometimes, it is not as simple as avoiding one or two talking *snakes*. Unfortunately, there are instances when a person with power and/or a group of people are not only negative but try to intimidate others. We have spoken to teachers who feel that either their administrator or a certain group of teachers targets them and more or less bullies them.

When addressing the issue of bullying in schools, people are generally referring to the students, but it can also happen with adults. According to the Workplace Bullying Institute, the term *workplace bullying* encompasses a pretty wide range of situations, but in general, it refers to repeated, health-harming mistreatment of an employee by one or more employees that can include verbal abuse, offensive nonverbal behaviors, or interfering with someone's ability to get work done. We are referring to actions that go beyond mere disapproval or general incivility. We are talking about grown-ups who pursue other grown-ups in order to do harm (Workplace Bullying Institute [WBI], 2022).

One teacher told us that because she chose to meet with troubled students during her lunch period, she was approached by a group of union members who told her they had worked hard to negotiate an unencumbered lunch period for all teachers and she was making the rest of them look bad. They asked her to stop doing job-related tasks during lunch, but she refused. Several of her colleagues decided to *shun* her after that. They would not look at her, speak to her, answer her, or in any way acknowledge her presence. She was left out of conversations. She was not invited to events—such as a baby shower, an after-school celebration for one of her retiring team members, and even an end-of-the-year party held in a neighboring teacher's home. She said that shunning was a common way for a powerful clique of teachers to keep others in line. She tried to talk about it to her administrator, but his reaction was, "Well, you know there's really no law against people not treating you the way you'd like. Maybe you should just try a little harder to get along with them." She was miserable at her school and transferred as soon as she was able.

It is true that there is no law against incivility or less aggressive forms of bullying in the workplace, but its effect can be destructive and devastating for all involved. Often, we are asked, "But what if that negative person is your boss? How can I minimize the effect of a negative superior? Good question. One young teacher lamented to us about her experience with her principal, whom she described as "the terminator on steroids."

> She never has a positive word to say to me. When I try to talk to her she doesn't look up from her smart phone she's tapping on. She writes me up for stuff that she lets her favorites get away with. I teach 110 percent most of the time, and the one time I was a little off and gave the kids a free period, she came to observe. She ripped me up one side and down the other on my evaluation. Her pet teacher gives free periods almost every week. She puts me on more committees than anyone else, makes sure I have at least 4 preps every year, and gives me the worst possible duty schedule. She ignores the grants I've gotten for this school, the awards I have for teaching, and the fact that I was just voted "My Favorite Teacher" by the students. She didn't even congratulate me on being selected.

> Last week she yelled at me for not turning in a form on time, but she didn't even put it in my box until the afternoon before it was due. I left early that day to go to a meeting she volunteered me for, so I never even saw it until it was already past due.

> I work harder than any teacher at this school, and no one cares. Sometimes I think I should show up at the last possible minute, do only the minimal work some of the other teachers do, and leave the second school is out. She hates me, and she is doing everything she can to make me leave. (Teacher prefers to remain anonymous.)

We would never tell a victim of bullying, "Even when people are bullying you, you can choose not to feel bad about it. Just remember to let a smile be your umbrella." (Gag. Choke.) We know that being bullied causes feelings of frustration and helplessness, an increased sense of vulnerability, tension, and stress. It leads to low morale and decreased productivity. It is a serious issue. Our advice to anyone in this situation is to adhere to Deliberate Optimism Principle #2, establish what you can control and seek tools and strategies to help you maximize your power. It applies in cases of oppression.

Determine What You Can and Cannot Control

What you cannot control

- How others choose to feel about you
- How others do their jobs
- The friendliness or the lack of friendliness people demonstrate toward you
- Assignments given to you by a superior

What you can control

- How you react to others
- How you do your job
- How you treat others
- How you handle what you are given
- What steps you take to alleviate the problem

There are definite steps you can take to alleviate the problem. Some people would suggest that you seek help from a superior. We think that should be your last step. Before reporting to the bully's boss, you might try some of these solutions:

1. Remember that it is not fun to pick on someone who refuses to be victimized. If a group of teachers is ignoring you, pretend you don't realize you're being ignored. Talk to them as if nothing is wrong, smile and wave when you see them, and continue to act oblivious to their exclusions. They may get tired of trying to shun you.

2. Find an ally to stand with you. It's much easier to ignore hateful people when you are not alone. (And it's especially helpful if your friend is the coach who used to play linebacker in the NFL.)

3. Make the perpetrator take responsibility for her actions. "Cruella, you failed to tell me the team was having a meeting this afternoon. Did you do that because you are angry with me for making that comment about your mock kiwi brownies?"

4. If a colleague or an administrator criticizes you, try to see if there is any merit to the accusation, and agree to work on it. Too often we hear teachers argue, "But everyone else was doing it," or "You never say anything to Mr. Socrates when he does that." First and foremost, we need to do what is right by our students. If giving a free period is not pedagogically sound, then it is wrong no matter who else is doing it. The best response to some reprimands is, "You are right. I will correct that," or "I hear what you are saying. I'll work on it."

5. Confront the bully on neutral ground and calmly say, "Look Voldemort, I've been upset by some things that happened lately like . . ." (specifically list your perceptions about occurrences that have troubled you). Perhaps try the words, "Help me understand what happened here." Don't attribute motive to the oppressor. Just quietly state the facts and report how you feel about it. If there is more than one person involved, choose the least confrontational person to speak with.

6. Make sure that you are not opening yourself up for criticism. It doesn't matter how great a teacher you are, if you are habitually late for school, meetings, or class, you give others an opening to complain. Be professional, be respectful, and be vigilant about doing your job assignments. No matter what others in your building are doing, quietly and diligently take care of all your school business before you try to defend yourself. "Okay, I might have been thirty minutes late for my first class, but I stayed here and worked last night until midnight," is no defense.

7. Start keeping private, accurate records of every action and communication from those involved. We're not suggesting that you become Deep Throat or a covert agent. Just document dates, times, what is said, what is done, and so forth. Leave out personal feelings, but as clearly and succinctly as possible, record what is said and done by all parties (including you). Reviewing your notes may help you put a different perspective on what is going on. Also, bullies are often articulate, manipulative, and calculating. They can sometimes paint a very different picture than what you convey, even sometimes making it appear that you are the perpetrator rather than the victim. Having accurate records will help you state your case to them or to the next level of management.

Having tried other means, you may feel that you have no choice but to appeal to an administrator for help. If, as in the case of the teacher who worked through lunch, your immediate superior is unwilling or incapable of helping, go to the next level. If the bully *is* your immediate superior, go to the next rank beyond them (their boss). When you make your case, stick to the facts. The argument, "I work harder than anyone in this school," holds little sway if the principal found you asleep at your desk during your third-period chemistry lab. Let your virtues speak for themselves. Reminding people that you were voted *The Best Second-Grade Remedial Reading Teacher for Period 4* (out of two candidates) is really not necessary and does not strengthen your case. Mary Kay Ash used to say, "Nothing wilts more quickly than a laurel rested upon." Just be confident that you are doing the best you can in the situation you are in every day for your students. Don't be afraid to ask the grown-ups at school to stop hindering that process. See more ideas for improving interpersonal relationships in Appendix 6.1.

●●● DISCUSSION QUESTIONS AND ACTION STEPS

1. Read the poem "Life Is a Theatre" in Appendix 6.2 and discuss how it relates to this chapter.

2. Name things that coworkers do or don't do that drain the enthusiasm and optimism right out of you. What can you do about your loss of spirit when that happens?

3. Do you consider yourself generally an extrovert or an introvert? Give examples of why you see yourself that way.

4. Do you have introverts on your staff? What steps should school leaders and other teachers take to make sure introverts feel valued and appreciated?

5. According to the Generations Chart, which generation do you belong to? Do you manifest the traits ascribed to your generation in this chapter? Explain your answer.

6. How have you handled *talking snakes* in the past? Discuss which methods in this chapter you are considering trying. What other ideas do you have about how to avoid *joy-depleters*?

7. Discuss the issue of bullying as it applies to the adults in your school. Give an example of a time you felt bullied or witnessed bullying in the workplace. What did you do about it? Were you satisfied with the outcome? Would you do something differently now? Why or why not?

8. What advice would you give to a teacher who confided in you that they feel bullied by one of the administrators on campus?

9. Describe a conflict at school among adults in which you were directly involved. What was your role in it? What was the outcome? Would you do anything differently if you could do it over again? Why or why not?

10. Read Appendix 6.1 "Ten Tips for Improving Interpersonal Relationships." As a group, decide which five are the most important. Discuss why. Have each group member write one additional way to get along better with others.

Action Steps for School Leaders

1. If you know there is a bully in your building, but you can't cut them from your roster (they probably bully you, too), avoid punishing that person with onerous duties. Instead, follow the advice in this chapter. You will be a good role model for others and refusing to be bullied is a great way to irritate the perpetrator.

2. Listen carefully when someone brings a complaint or conflict involving another person on staff. Ask yourself if this is something you need to solve or if the two people can work it out themselves with a bit of guidance.

3. Acknowledge that your faculty and staff must deal with difficult people both within the school community and beyond. Offer occasional articles or brief seminars to help teachers deal with some of these irritants. Just showing that you are aware of the situation and care about those who are affected can go a long way.

4. Plan a faculty outing to a roller rink, a bowling alley, a paintball facility, Topgolf, or some other kind of entertainment venue that will have participants moving and interacting. Probably some won't come, but that's okay. Those who show up will have a terrific time.

5. Ask staff members to provide you with pictures of themselves when they were the age of the students they teach. Display them where both staff and students can see them, and let people see how many they can match to the adults at school. You can even make it a contest and award prizes.

6. Encourage positive, cheery teachers to "adopt" a cynical colleague. Have them make it a point to reach out to that person, do thoughtful things for that person, and try to help that person feel more a part of the school community. Be sure to privately acknowledge and offer support to your "Cheer Fairies."

As we watch some of our colleagues down sad and angry paths, try to help them, but also find those who haven't gone there yet. Smiles will help keep you aloft, even if the solutions to greater problems are still in progress.

—Wolpert-Gawron (2013), middle school teacher, author, blogger

BUILDING A POSITIVE SHARED SCHOOL COMMUNITY

Relatedness

....

For schools to thrive, teachers and leaders should feel the confidence of self-determination. Earlier chapters explore two of the factors in self-determination theory—autonomy and competence. The third component, relatedness, involves feelings of belonging to a particular group. Without connections, self-determination is harder to achieve because individuals lack access to the support that comes from affiliation. To build a positive shared community for students, teachers, staff, leaders, support personnel, and everyone involved in a school, relationships must be intentionally built and fostered.

We need to work together for the common good as well as for our own good. Education can no longer support a system whose professionals operate in isolation.

> Many teachers continue to work largely alone in classrooms, and many schools still have essentially the same "egg-crate" structure first described by historian, David Tyack and sociologist Dan Lortie over forty years ago. But should they? In no other field is the basic organization of professional work as spare and rudimentary as in school. Professionals working in other large-scale enterprise—for example, health management organizations, banks, and technology companies—are not left on their own to develop their skills, devise their strategies, and serve their clients as they see fit. (Johnson, 2019, p. 4)

In most successful schools we have worked in and visited, we have found these collective attributes—a common vision, a shared values system, effective communication among all personnel, demonstrated mutual respect, and a sense of optimism. Along with these attributes, great schools have trust within the building and the capacity to hold each other accountable. Schools with those characteristics in place generally have the efficacy required to face adversity with perseverance and resilience.

In speaking about developing and instilling resilience in others, author and poet Maya Angelou says,

> I'm not sure if resilience is ever achieved alone. Experience allows us to learn from example. But if we have someone who loves us—I don't mean who indulges us, but who loves us enough to be on our side—then it's easier to grow resilience, to grow belief in self, to grow self-esteem. And it's self-esteem that allows a person to stand up. (Azzam, 2013, p. 10)

Dr. Angelou is primarily talking about building resiliency in children through their families, but we think her words are also true for the school community. School communities need to function as family units, and we the teachers, too, need to stand by each other, encourage each other, and demand the best of each other. We believe that all the adults at school should stand together. (Even though we are outnumbered by the kids, at least standing together gives us a fighting chance.)

Collective Efficacy

Feeling a part of a trusted group can lead to the desirable state of *collective efficacy*. Chapter 1 talks about how individual efficacy (the belief that one can produce a desired or intended result) is an integral part of realistic optimism. In groups that feel a sense of belonging and camaraderie, there can be a shared efficacy (power in numbers). Bandura (2009) believes that *collective efficacy* (which he calls *organizational agency*) involves using the combined beliefs of a group of individuals to act as a whole to achieve a desired action or result.

Involving teachers in all aspects of curriculum planning and implementation not only empowers them but also better ensures their support of the overall goals.

> When teachers are on instructional leadership teams . . . , a sense of community is built along with the important instructional work being done. Teachers feel a shared sense of responsibility to one another

and to the students. Being able to see and interact with schoolwide data helps teachers break out of their classroom perspective and begin to better see where their piece fits into the big picture. (DiTullio, 2022)

Teams can be composed of a few like minds, a small group, a whole school, or even an entire community. A whole school approach focuses on the contributions of members across the school community, usually to ensure all students have the opportunity to maximize their learning experience. Whatever the goal calls for determines who the participants should be.

School Uses a Team Approach to Solve Behavior Problems

At Martin Luther King Jr. Academic Middle School in San Francisco, teachers suffered burnout from behavior issues. Disengaged learners created constant disruptions to avoid classwork. Teacher–student relationships plummeted.

The principal, deans, and counselors wanted teachers to practice restorative practices at the time of the disruption but realized it was unrealistic to expect teachers to stop instruction and deal effectively with recurring interruptions. As an alternative solution, the team assigned support staff—adults who did not have teaching roles (e.g., social workers, deans, academic advisors)—to go into classrooms to help with disturbances.

After training teachers in deescalation practices, they formed a rotating "push in" system whereby some of the non-teaching staff were always available via walkie talkie to respond to a teacher's request for assistance. They either took over the class while the teacher met privately with the student, or they met privately with the student while the teacher continued instruction. Behavior improved dramatically with this team approach (Baker, 2017).

Team Teaching, Revisited

An innovative approach addressing teacher shortages, staff morale, and declining enrollment has been piloted in some Mesa, Arizona, schools. The idea is quickly catching on around the state and beyond. Volunteer teachers in elementary through high school are putting sometimes 100 or more students and four or more teachers in one giant classroom. Teacher teams meet for two hours each morning to plan personalized programs for every student as they map out their rotations from big-group instruction, one-on-one interventions, small study groups, and more. Teachers praise the added benefit of extended comradeship among themselves, and students say they feel more connected to the teachers and the school. Teachers who participate in the team approach report improved morale and better-quality opportunities for professional growth. Promising results show greater retention of students and staff (Morton, 2022).

The *Stay* Interview

We love to read about original ideas school districts are willing to try—especially when they work. We are all aware that teachers are leaving the profession in unprecedented numbers. Perhaps it is time to rethink how we retain our excellent educators. Most of us are quite familiar with the *exit interview*, which asks a departing staff member why they are leaving and what the school or district could have done better to retain them. Exit interviews are not always that helpful because those leaving usually have little motivation to spend time recapping why they chose to leave. It doesn't help retain a valuable employee.

Human resources expert Emily Beck has proposed a new interview called the *stay interview* (Heubeck, 2022). In her work with Maricopa County in Arizona, Beck has helped develop a tool kit for conversations with the district's top performers, flight risks, and high potential staff members. In a one-to-one interview, selected educators are brought in to give voice to their reasons for staying. In thirty to forty minutes, interviewees are asked about what motivates and frustrates them and what they would like to see changed.

Example questions might include the following:

- What do you look forward to when you come to work each day?

- If you were to consider leaving this position, why would that be?

- What factors might trigger a departure?

The district likes to conduct the interviews early in the year so that they have time to address concerns raised by the interviewees. They know it is important to let teachers know they take their concerns seriously and will work on the issues mentioned. Beck says an effective stay interview can elicit powerful information from employees considered to be "enthusiastic stayers." In turn, they can use their input to ensure the teachers' continued job engagement and retention. Since the inception of the stay interviews, the retention rate at Maricopa County Schools has exceeded 90 percent in an area that generally has one of the worst teacher retention rates in the country. What an inspired idea this is for reinforcing collective efficacy!

SEL for Grown-Ups

Building strong relationships among all participants supports optimism. It's not always easy to combine a group of diverse people into a cohesive unit. Teachers have been trying to manage this task in their classrooms for years. In the last few years, there has been a growing interest in social-emotional learning (SEL) for students. Time taken to teach and practice self-smart and people-smart skills is yielding positive social and academic gains in schools across the country.

We think it is time to capitalize on the benefits of SEL training and practice for the entire school community. A positive school culture starts with the adult relationships on campus. Intentional professional development and mutual support can tremendously advance the joy of working at school. Key elements of professional social-emotional competence are the ability to practice self-awareness and self-management, make responsible decisions, maintain and grow relationships, and practice social awareness (Collaborative for Academic, Social, and Emotional Learning [CASEL], 2022). Focusing on these areas of growth can make us stronger together.

Why not implement adult versions of SEL activities monthly? At staff meetings, participants can practice the same SEL activities they have their students do then reflect on what they learned about the activity, themselves, and each other. Valuable aspects of community building can also provide informal interactions with great fun when the participants go on retreats together, meet outside the school setting for games or adventures, gather in social settings, or participate in special event days at school (e.g., favorite university apparel day, "freaky hair" day, dress as your favorite fictional character day). There are massive amounts of ideas for SEL activities available, and most of them cost little or nothing to implement. See Appendix 7.1 for more ideas. Following is a frequently used activity that demonstrates how making mistakes together is an effective way to building a cohesive partnership.

1–2–3 Clap Game

SEL Skills: Self-management; relationship building

Instructions

Round 1

- Ask participants to find a partner (or partner them up in a way that is appropriate for your group). Note: The same partners face each other during each of the three rounds.

- Explain that pairs will count to three over and over again, with partners alternating saying the next number in the sequence.

- Model slowly with a partner.

- Once everyone has had a minute or two to play, use your attention signal to bring that round to a close.

- Ask: *How many of you made a mistake? What did you do when you made a mistake?* (Typical answers are "Laughed," or said, "Sorry," or pulled back.)

- Explain that these are all ways that people give cues to the group that say, "I've got this. I'll laugh at myself or apologize so you won't push me out."

- Tell the group that during the next round, when someone makes a mistake, they should raise their hands in the air and say, "Ta-da!"

Round 2

- Explain that for this round, pairs should replace the number "1" with a clap and then continue the number sequence "2, 3" counted out loud (Clap, 2, 3; Clap, 2, 3; etc.).

- Model slowly with a partner. During the modeling, purposefully make a mistake such as saying "1" instead of clapping after "3." Raise your hands in the air and say, "Ta-da!"

- Once everyone has had a minute or two to play, call the round to a close. Ask: *Was anyone glad that they weren't the only one making a mistake?*

- Tell the group that in the next round when one person makes a mistake, both partners will raise their hands in the air, give each other a double high-five, and both say, "Ta-da!"

Round 3

- Explain that in this round, pairs should clap for "1," replace the number "2" with a foot stomp, and say "3." (Clap, stomp, 3; Clap, stomp, 3; etc.).

- Model this with a partner and purposefully make a mistake, such as saying "2" instead of stomping. You and your partner now give each other double high-fives and shout, "Ta-da!" together, and start over again.

- Once everyone has had a minute or two to play, call the round to a close.

- Ask participants to notice how they were taking care of each other and were learning to sync with each other—finding the right pace for everyone to succeed.

- Ask participants to notice the positive energy that was created with each mistake in the group. Explain that when they work together from now on, they should try to keep that same energy when mistakes are made. Ta-da!

Closure

- With a partner, in small groups, or as a whole group ask participants what SEL skills were reinforced with this activity

- Ask the group for reflections about doing activities like these as a staff.

When Conflicts Arise

Short games can be a lot of fun, but whenever humans come into contact for long periods of time, conflicts naturally arise. Some are easily smoothed over by a simple, "I'm sorry, those were my hormones talking in the meeting yesterday." Others require more effort to amend. Nearly every school now offers training for students in conflict resolution. Unfortunately, many teachers pay little attention to it for themselves. When conflicts arise among colleagues, some of us sulk, pout, offer reprisals, or generally act worse than the students we teach.

Unresolved disagreements inhibit any kind of ongoing productivity in the educational setting, but especially among teammates. When conflicts arise, they should be dealt with immediately rather than be allowed to fester. Just as they do with their parents, students easily perceive animosity among teachers (even before the dartboard with the offending teacher's picture on it goes up inside your storage closet). All the positive thinking in the world won't cover up a single rancorous dispute among colleagues. For some teachers, compliance or compromise is the easy answer, but often contention and resentment remain so there is no real resolution.

The realistic optimist believes in the importance of positive thinking but is often stymied by the lack of positive energy on the part of other adults in the building. Beaten down by the negative input described in earlier chapters, many educators have lost the will to be friendly and approachable or even a teeny bit social.

Administrators are equally overworked. Developing a fun and favorable school climate often falls low on their priority list. It is up to the deliberate optimists to make inroads. We often have to be intentional in constructing positive experiences in order to remain hopeful.

Building Positive Relationships With Your Colleagues

Principle 3 of deliberate optimism requires that we do something positive toward our goal. We have seen many schools implement powerful strategies to help the adults at school work in an encouraging, cooperative manner. Here are a few general ideas to get you started toward building positive relationships with your colleagues:

- Start small. Find out what you have in common with one or two teachers on your team or in your curricular area. Build on those commonalities, then reach out to a few more teachers.

- Find something in common with the Eeyore on your team or in the building. Build on that. Maybe you both liked the movie *Top Gun: Maverick* (2022) or hated *Transformers* or love cold pizza (you've seen them stealing it out of the lounge fridge) or prefer to sit in the back on PD days.

- Don't deny that there are stressors in your work (the Pollyanna personality is pretty annoying) but continue to point out—and act out—ways in which you can overcome those stress points in areas where you have control.

- Do at least one unexpected, nice thing for each team member each month—a note, a flower for their desk, or a bit of verbal support when they're down. If your team is already in sync, use this plan for others in the building who need to be lifted out of their pessimism.

- Don't gossip. Just DON'T. Gossip never helps. It only makes conflicts worse. (Remember what your mama always told you, "Less said, better done.")

- Support your administrator and keep them in the loop. Even if you disagree with a decision, agree to disagree in private.

- Commit yourself to loyalty—to your class, your team, your administrators, and the school. You are seen as the "authority" in your community—build optimism not defeatism. (See Appendix 7.3 Loyalty.)

I am a secondary science teacher. When my late husband was diagnosed with terminal cancer, I wanted to spend as much time with him as I could. I used up all of my sick days, and expenses were tight. My peers made a schedule of my classes and volunteered to teach during their prep periods so that I would not have to pay a sub, and my students wouldn't suffer in my absence. They took over and made sure my students had solid learning experiences while I was at my husband's bedside. My gratitude to them is beyond measure. I cannot imagine teaching in a school where staff members do not support one another.

—J.P. Science teacher, Shreveport, LA.

Action Step 7.2

HOW TO SET BOUNDARIES AND STOP PEOPLE PLEASING

Scan QR Code 7.2 to watch the 9.5-minute video, *How to Set Boundaries and Stop People Pleasing.* Were there any "aha" moments for you in this clip? Did you hear anything that affirmed what you already believe and practice?

Advice for Teaming

Judith Baenen and Jack Berckemeyer give specific pointers on making meetings with colleagues successful. They offer the following advice.

Advice for Teaming (for Teams or Departments)

1. Pledge to be on time and stay until the end.

2. Give the meeting your full attention; do not grade papers or check your score on *Candy Crush.*

3. If you have an opinion, share it at the meeting, not at a *meeting after the meeting.*

4. Listen respectfully to others' ideas and opinions. Try to see their point of view.

5. Don't take conflict personally.

6. Once a decision is made, try to go with it even if you disagree.

What Can You Live With?
....

In his book, *Taming of the Team: How Great Teams Work Together,* Berckemeyer (2012) presents an excellent strategy for resolving conflicts among team members. When teams are having difficulty reaching consensus, they can ask each other the question, "What can you live with?" In other words, he gives teachers the responsibility of making a decision while still offering them ownership of its consequences. A team member might say something like, "I don't like the idea of not letting the students go back to their lockers after each class change, but I can live with restricting visits to the lockers during lunch."

There will always be teachers who seem to "march to the beat of a different drummer." Yes, we're talking about Ms. Bliss who skips, prances, and bakes brownies. She is an amazing example of how educators can remain joyful even in the darkest of times. And for each Priscilla Perfect and Mr. Magical, we should be grateful because they're the ones who know that true hope, passion, and optimism still resonate within the confines of a school building. (Plus, they are the ones who bring the all the baked goods, help us get organized, and provide innovative ideas.) Principle 4 of deliberate optimism, Own It, requires us to be more authentic in our relationships with the other adults at school. We need to support one another and help each other grow toward being our very best selves.

Build a Relationship Culture That Includes Students

The goal is to create a *relationship culture* that is embedded into the climate of the school. It is not something that is done overnight. It takes time, commitment, and strong leadership. Relationship culture is just as important as the academic rigor that schools strive to achieve. Time needs to be spent with the entire staff to help them understand that there is a process and belief in how we treat each other, the parents and caregivers of our students, the student themselves, and guests who enter the building. A relationship culture is also taught and practiced by the students within the building.

This culture is not just observed by good deeds and kindness but by support and respect for each other. Students want and crave a place that is fair and consistent. For many of our students, school is the only place for them to be treated fairly by the adults and by other students. And let's be truthful, in many cases, educators are the most stable person in some of our students' lives. (We know that this might be shocking to you as you look around the room during a faculty meeting. Some of your coworkers may not seem even close to stable.)

The easier tasks within a school tend be teaching strategies and mastering new educational concepts. The more difficult tasks are the ones in which we are asked to change our over-all beliefs about the adults in the building. To be blunt, there are some teachers who choose to remain in the classroom for the wrong reasons, and they have created a culture that not only lacks optimism but also is devoid of even moderately civil encounters with students. Teaching critical thinking skills, essential ideas, and self-efficacy begins with the process of building relationships with students.

> *Never close your door to collaboration. You know how they say that moving elderly people into the hospital can quicken their demise? Closing your door to colleagues is rather like that. The act begins to deteriorate your ability to see the good. When you close the door, you are moving access to positive practices into hospice care.*
>
> —Wolpert-Gawron (2013), middle school teacher, blogger

Ideas in Building a Relationship Culture

1. Greet students every day as they enter the building. This might mean assigning some teachers and administrators to the main entrances of the school. Some schools greet the students and the parents as they drop their students off in front of the building. We have even seen an administrator and a teacher greet every student when the bus pulls up into the parking lot. (And yes, the educators in the building also wave even more vigorously as the bus leaves school at the end of the day.) Greeting students helps set the tone for the day and helps with security issues. It allows the staff to check on the tone and attitude of students as they enter the building.

2. As students enter the building and are greeted, the teachers and administrative team can make sure that every student is also, "ready to learn." This might mean a reminder that the student's shirt needs to be tucked in, the hoodie taken off, the hat removed, and the pants pulled up. (Added note: Do you know what the longest educational trend has ever been? Sagging pants! We are going on over 35 years of sagging pants. Heck, *Common Core* did not even last that long!)

3. Expect all teachers to be visible in the hallways saying "hello" to students. They do this by their classroom doors and in the hallways. In our observations in schools, we have noted that some educators refuse to greet or even acknowledge students. In our opinion, this is an example of *educational criminality* and is further evidence that we need to police our own ranks by letting all adults in the building know it is not an acceptable practice to ignore kids. In all fairness, we know that school has become the whipping boy of society and that educators are tired of being bashed. But here is the reality—whatever is happening to us is not the fault of a student. A seven-, eleven-, or sixteen-year-old did not put us in this situation. We can start by saying "hello" to our students in the hallways, it is the least we can do!

4. Ask the educators in the building to create an oath or an agreement on what it means to be an educator or leader in the building. This could mean that there is a list of statements that everyone agrees to. Decide a simple and easy way to make each of the statements visible and recognizable. In other words, what ways do we see teachers greeting students and how do we hold each other accountable when that does not happen? The easy part is making the list; the hard part is holding each other accountable.

5. Making sure every student has an adult advocate also helps create a relationship culture.

6. Change or enhance the culture and climate of school regarding relationships so that every adult has a chance to know every other adult in a meaningful way. For some schools, this means putting a picture of each teacher on a bulletin board from when they were in elementary, middle, or high school. We also encourage adults to display their educational backgrounds as well. (Yes, it is okay to flaunt your degrees and achievements. Every other profession does it, and we should, too.)

We Are Advocates for Students

Not only can teachers and school leaders act collectively to address the deep roots of social problems in our schools, but we can also act individually, starting with our own classes. Something as simple as the classic sociogram can be so effective, yet how many of us now take the time to look at how our students fit in the school or classroom culture? How many of us make the time to forge those important relationships not only among students but also with us? Believe it or not, teachers in PreK all the way through grade 12 are very important to their students.

Students of all ages need adults in their lives who pay attention to them, listen to them, and point them in the right direction. Sometimes, a brief greeting or question about how the day is going is all that is required to let students know they are valued and that they belong. Occasionally, students need the help of an adult to solve a problem, to make a plan, or just to get some guidance. Depending on the grade, maturity, and skill levels of the kid, educators can step in when necessary to offer an assist.

Scenario 1

A student's advocate goes to bat for him because they understand what is at stake.

Jeremy enters the homeroom, tosses his backpack on the floor, and slumps in his chair.

"What's up?" you ask.

"I studied for my stupid science test today, and mean Ms. Pipette wouldn't let me take it because I didn't have a blue pen."

"Gosh, Jeremy, I'm sorry about that. I know you really studied, and when we went over that study sheet this morning, you knew it all."

"Yeah, but a fat lot of good that did! Why should I even study?"

"Look, Jeremy, I'm going to talk with Ms. Pipette and see if you can't take the test after all. I don't want you to give up on studying. I'll explain that next time you will have your required materials."

Scenario 2

A student's advocate assists the student in navigating the everyday problems of being a student.

Mr. Sonnet is waiting in the locker hall when Liza arrives after the final bell for the day. He greets her as she begins to unload her backpack.

"What's for homework tonight, Liza?"

"I don't know—probably math. I don't know."

"How about we look at your planner and see if you wrote anything down for tonight?"

"Okay, if you want to."

"Well, it looks as if you have math and some reading to do in science. You'd better get your science book out of your locker—er, no,—that's your Spanish book; the science book is the blue one."

"Oh, yeah."

"Hey, it looks like you have a history quiz tomorrow. History notes go in the backpack, too."

"Okay. Thanks, Mr. Sonnet. Lots of times I don't get home with the right stuff. Thanks for helping me."

While we want all students to eventually evolve into self-sufficient independent thinkers, there are many times they need an adult to help them stay on the path to maturity. The willingness of educators to advocate for students is an indicator of a positive school community.

Building Student-to-Student Relationships

Sometimes, students can be malicious and brutal to each other. Sometimes, their actions are erratic and beyond explanation. They can kick their best friend's backpack all the way down the hall while calling him names then drop a dollar into the charity bucket for the tsunami relief effort. Many would say that schools and classrooms are like survival of the fittest. The powerful pounce on the weak, and the weak either take the abuse or complain to the adult in the room. The cycle of distrust and disrespect must be addressed and changed to create a positive relationship culture.

The best place to start is by creating a classroom that is warm and inviting to each of our students. It is also a place where disrespect will be addressed and dealt with in a calm and realistic manner. For example, anytime a student is being disrespectful to another student or there is a conflict in the classroom, many teachers (pre-COVID) asked that the students not only apologize but also shake each other's hands. The power of the handshake is a lost art that still has symbolic and life-affirming attributes.

Some teachers have their students create guidelines on how to treat each other. They also ask class member to figure out ways to hold each other accountable. Remember that the lists are easy to create; the action items and accountability are the difficult part. See Appendix 7.2 Student Accountability for examples.

Creating a positive relationship classroom culture is no easy task. There are many commercial programs now available to help schools improve their school climates; however, we don't believe it's about any program, no matter how well packaged. It is about knowing our students, letting them get to know us, and making sure our students feel welcomed when they enter the building and our classrooms.

For years, we (authors) along with others have said that student learning starts with relationships. The deliberate optimist speaks up and says that schools should be safe havens for emotionally battered students as well as those who are well adjusted, and it is we as teachers who are called to create those sanctuaries. We accept the fact that content is critical; yet relationship building is life changing. If we truly want to reclaim the joy in education, we need to be at least as deliberately attentive to students' social emotional issues as we are to the academic ones.

Action Step 7.3

RELATIONSHIP BUILDING: GETTING TO KNOW YOUR STUDENTS

Scan QR Code 7.3 to watch the 3-minute, video, *Relationship Building: Getting to Know Your Students* featuring teachers in San Bernadino. Think of the things you purposefully do to build relationships with your students (no matter what age group you teach).

••• DISCUSSION QUESTIONS AND ACTION STEPS

1. What is the general quality of faculty relationships on your campus? Do you feel valued and appreciated by your colleagues? Why or Why not?

2. What evidence can you cite (it can be anecdotal or something you've read) that supports the authors' assertion that building positive relationships with students supports higher achievement?

3. Discuss the piece, "Loyalty" by Elbert Hubbard (Appendix 7.3) and relate it to how teachers and school leaders should support their schools. Do you agree with what Hubbard says?

4. What did you think about the whole school approach to behavior initiated by a school leader and his administrative team at MLK Middle School in San Francisco? What are the accepted guidelines for behavior management in your school? Do all staff members stand united on the plan? Should they?

5. What are the benefits of conducting *Stay* interviews? Would you like to be part of one? Why or why not?

6. Discuss your reaction to the chapter's advice about teaming. What suggestions are you and your team or department already doing? Which suggestions would not work for you? Why not? Name a suggestion you would like to try and tell why.

7. What are some of the ways you make every student feel welcome in your classroom?

8. Outside the classroom, how do you continue to act as an advocate for your students?

9. Do you think you are a good team member? Why or why not?

10. Name your favorite team-building activity for grown-ups. Tell why you like it and describe how it would work in a faculty meeting at your school. See if you can get your school leader to try it.

Action Steps for School Leaders

1. Provide a detailed weekly memo from the administrative team. This is a great place to add details about upcoming events, give props to staff that went above and beyond, mention birthdays and special events, celebrate good things going on at your school, and reflect on overall goals and school philosophy.

2. With teachers, establish common goals and protocols for team and department meetings. Drop by their meetings from time to time just to observe the dynamics and to answer questions. Send them a note praising their positive interactions.

3. Occasionally, start professional development activities and faculty meetings with team-building activities that are fun. Plan it so that people have a chance to interact with different colleagues each time. Ask teachers to suggest SEL activities that would be beneficial for faculty members.

4. Ask teachers to take one day during the year to shadow a student. Provide a substitute for the teacher and ask them to follow a student around for a full day from the bus ride to school to the bus ride home.

(Continued)

(Continued)

> They should keep a journal throughout the day and spend most of their time listening and watching their chosen student. Have the observing teacher write about the experience, talk to you about it, share with their colleagues, and/or talk with other appropriate staff about what they learned.

5. In a faculty meeting, bring up the topic of student advocacy. Discuss with teachers what you think advocacy means in terms of the grade levels of the students in your school. Brainstorm with teachers a list of "non-negotiables" about practices for interacting with students on your campus.

6. Set up a few role-play situations regarding teachers interacting with students. Draw names or select faculty members to take on the roles of students and teachers. Read a scenario and ask the actors to demonstrate what they would do in certain situations. After the role play, ask audience members to offer opinions about what they saw and contribute ideas for other ways to handle the situation. Move on to the next scenario.

7. Drop in on classes on an informal basis as often as possible. Ask students about their work and let them show you what they are doing and tell you what they are learning. In joyful schools when administrators enter a room, the momentum is unchanged. Students and teachers are comfortable with having their principals "join the fun."

8. Use social networking to arrange drop-ins from former students.

> Let them surprise former teachers with a visit and perhaps a note of appreciation.

9. Set up something like a "Secret Pal" society whereby each staff member anonymously affirms another staff member with small treats, positive notes, and thoughtful deeds. The secret pals can remain the same for a holiday season, a semester, or the year. Have a Reveal Party at the end of the time period so that identities can be revealed, and a random drawing can be held to select new pals for the next time period. Don't forget to put your name in the drawing. (And don't assume this won't work in high school. We have seen it work splendidly with secondary teachers.)

JOYFUL SCHOOL COMMUNITIES—THE SUM OF THEIR PARTS

When we become a really mature, grown-up, wise society, we will put teachers at the center of the community, where they belong. We don't honor them enough, we don't pay them enough.

—Charles Kuralt

In *The Power of Professional Capital*, Hargreaves and Fullan (2013) write about increasing professional capital to improve education in the United States. They are referring to a practice of elevating the teaching profession across the board with higher pay, more autonomy, more trust, more time for professional development, and more attention to retaining an experienced, excellent workforce. They state that countries like Finland, Singapore, and Canada develop the whole profession rather than focusing on removing the few at the bottom or rewarding only those at the top. Hargreaves and Fullan maintain that government bodies need to demonstrate courage and faith in investing in teacher development and empowerment.

> To attract people to the profession, you need a good set of schools for those people to work in. Continuous professional development pays off in Finland, Singapore, Alberta, and Ontario. The best way you can support and motivate teachers is to create the conditions where they can be effective day after day, together. And this isn't just about intraschool collaboration. It's about interschool and inter-district collaboration. It's about the whole profession. (Hargreaves & Fullan, 2013, p. 37)

It is good to read comments from people like social commentator the late Charles Kuralt as well as respected researchers Andy Hargreaves and Michael Fullan, who agree the teaching profession needs a new appreciation and perhaps a new focus. We would add that we think schools need to follow other top educational countries in providing teachers with unencumbered time during the school day to study, collaborate, and reflect on their practices. One reason U.S. teachers feel so overextended is that there is little or no time in their school day schedule for professional deliberations or personal growth.

We find promise and hope in what Jennifer D. Klein, director of educator development for the World Leadership School, writes:

> There are schools all over the world that are getting it right, building communities where teachers are trusted and enjoy their work, even feel empowered to do right by kids. There are even schools where students are central protagonists, trusted by the educators who work with them to manage more of their learning journey and articulate their own growth. Many districts are doing exceptional work to shift local policy, and new movements in place-based learning are reclaiming the rights of indigenous and marginalized communities to define their own educational systems and outcomes, how they believe achievement should be defined inside their schools. There are even entire countries building systems that rely on teachers to make most decisions about students' learning needs. (Klein, 2022)

For now, we urge all those involved in schools to follow the four principals of Deliberate Optimism and take the concrete steps we can to build a better educational system. Previous chapters focus on what teachers and leaders can do for themselves to reclaim their joy for education. We also want to address what teachers, administrators, parents, and local communities can do to help restore optimism and hope in our nation's schools.

Something to work toward—

All teachers, especially newer teachers, should teach no more than four hours a day and spend the other four hours a day on their own learning and in collaboration with colleagues. They might study data about student learning and develop strategies for how to respond, observe in a master teacher's classroom, or write lesson plans and common assessments. They might coach other teachers, write curriculum, do policy work, and lead professional development.

—Richardson (2013), editor in chief, *Kappan.*

The Administrators

Rafe Esquith believes that "School morale begins at the top, and when school leaders respect and believe in their teachers, everyone wins. Most staff members are more than willing to do some of the more unpleasant parts of their jobs because they work for a principal who rolls up his sleeves and works alongside them" (Esquith, 2014, p. 21).

Strasser (2014) interviewed principals and teachers in New York's Rochester City School District to ask about how administrators can help build and sustain teacher morale. Collectively, they came up with some interesting but probably not surprising advice for administrators.

How Administrators Can Boost Morale

1. First have the common courtesy to give teachers what they ask for. If a teacher asks to have a refrigerator in her room, why make her defend her reason? Why not just get one for her? When teachers say they need more paper, more books, or more science supplies, why not trust that they know what it takes to get the job done and move heaven and earth to make sure they have what they need? If the request is impossible, work on a suitable alternative with the teacher.

2. Communication cannot be emphasized strongly enough. Ironically, some of the world's worst communicators see themselves as extremely proficient in that area. Start by either you or your assistant routinely popping in and out of classes as part of the culture (rather than "I gotcha'!"). Be honest with teachers. If the district has told you to check that everyone's learning goals are on the board, be transparent and tell them, "Today I'll be dropping into everyone's rooms to check that your learning goals are written in the top right-hand corner of your board. Not my idea, by the way." Tell teachers as openly as you can about the complexities of running the school. Make it a point to know about staff members' situations, families, and other important personal data.

3. Treat teachers like adults. Give teachers autonomy and do not try to micromanage their lesson plans, emails, sick leave, or departure time from school. Involve them in planning their schedules and be flexible with them about attending to their own family needs. Work on the premise that as long as the work gets done, essential ideas are taught, and connections are made with kids and their families, teachers can have the flexibility to determine how they spend their time.

(Continued)

4. Play with the gray area. There is sometimes a tension between doing what the district wants and what is morally and ethically correct for teachers; err to the side of the teachers. Fight for your teachers and let them know you are doing just that.

5. Remember that morale is only a side effect. A former school superintendent wrote, "Teacher morale, in my experience, is not a function of practices designed to maintain or create it. It is a by-product of being treated as leaders and being treated with respect. Teacher morale is the end product of empowering teachers to make decisions that affect their lives."

Most teachers reading this chapter are now shouting, "Amen! Yes, that's what **They** should be doing." But let's be fair and make sure teachers do what they can to support leaders. Administrators are busy people. Whereas teachers must answer to our students and their families, administrators have many more constituents to connect with, including the teachers, the staff, all the families, the district officials, the school board, the broader community, and the secretary who runs the front office. Today's school principals and their assistants have truckloads of paperwork, endless meetings, and constantly evolving demands. Many administrators would love to be with the students more and would enjoy tossing around ideas on how to make the school a joyful environment, but they just don't see where they have the time.

Their minimal resource of extra time is why ideas the actions we wish to take toward building a positive school climate should be well thought out and involve as little effort on the part of the administrators as possible. It won't work well to say, "**You** should . . ." or "Why don't **you** . . .?" Instead, we need to prepare our plans beforehand and let the administrator know we will take the lead to do what needs to be done. We are just meeting with them to provide the necessary information and ensure it works with their school plan.

Ascribing it to many factors, teachers often admit they spend little time talking educational philosophy with peers. It is even more rare for teachers and administrators to spend time conversing philosophically about real educational issues. While some schools encourage teams to discuss books or articles together as part of their professional development, the administrators often have only enough time to sit briefly with a team before moving on to some crisis. We need to try and find a way to help our administrator(s) carve out some time to discuss our shared over-all school belief systems.

Remember, too, that administrators' lives are relatively lonely regarding their connection with school. We have our teammates and students to engage us each day—the administrators often have little else but problems and paperwork. Perhaps we teachers could occasionally send a little note of affirmation, a birthday/holiday remembrance, a random flower or treat on the desk, or a thank you for a specific deed. Everyone likes to be valued, and sometimes school leaders get left out of the mix. Remember, they are often caught in the middle. Everything from the district runs downhill to their desks, and everything at the school runs uphill to the same place. It's not usually a fun place to be.

And for goodness sake, we need to avoid the *talking snake* in the lounge who criticizes every move the administrator makes. Or maybe we need to go into the lounge and stick up for the person not there to defend themselves. Often these diatribes are founded on rumor or guilt perpetuated by dysfunctional people who obviously have not read our *Deliberate Optimism* book ☺.

When controversial issues come to light, go straight to the administrator to get the facts. Principle 1 of Deliberate Optimism is to gather as much information about the situation as possible. But be aware that a lot of what weighs heavily on the minds of administrators is information they cannot share with others, even in defense of themselves. They are privy to all kinds of private data about the central office, personnel, students, the parents, and more information than they want to know. They are obliged by professionalism not to discuss these matters, and perhaps we should be a little more tolerant about giving them the benefit of the doubt.

If, by chance, you have an administrator who is not really suited to run a joyful school, do what you can to work with and around them. This can usually be done without calling attention to the individual's deficits. Stick to the idea of planning ahead in order to make it easier for the administrator to say "yes" since there is little they are required to do to make your plan work. Support what you can. Be positive. Use the strength of your caucus (discussed later in this chapter). Bring along chocolate.

The Parents

You can never help a student by alienating their parents.

—Debbie Silver

We hope it does not surprise you to learn that the families of our students also want your school to be a warm, caring, and positive environment. Gallup Poll on Education (GALLUP, 2013) found that the adults surveyed thought teachers should be more caring and interested. Now before you get furious, reflect on all that we have said so far in this book. Perhaps you are reading this alone. Perhaps you are sharing it with your team or book group. But are you sharing it with the families of the children who attend your school? How can they know about what's bugging us or what it is we need, if we don't tell them? Who tells them about the novel ideas we have or strategies we think will enhance our classrooms or schools? How do they know about the countless hours we spend enhancing our skills and building our knowledge bases? If we don't tell them, who will?

Let's first deal with the families of the students we teach. You probably spend a lot of time connecting with parents—via classroom newsletter, email blasts, parent portal information, and so forth. If you are aware that not all your parents have computer access at home, you likely also use paper communication, phone calls, and so forth. Most teachers today believe they are communicating a lot of information all the time, and they are. On the other hand, it is evident that the connection is mostly one-way. Oh sure, you were wise enough to send out a sheet before school began asking parents to comment on their child's strengths and weaknesses, hopes and dreams, but then what?

What is missing is not *communication*; it's *conversation*. Conversation is two-sided, give and take, and alas, time consuming. But if you have friends, lovers, or a medical problem, you cannot deny the urgency and fruitlessness of a single-sided conversation. And this is often what is missing for us as educators when it comes to connecting with parents. We pour information out over them like a reservoir spillway and generally miss seeing them sputter and gurgle with the flow. One ten- or fifteen-minute conversation can make all the difference, especially for families who aren't used to navigating a large—or even small—school system.

When and where do we have these conversations? Let's start with an open house or return to school night. Make it a point to have two or three actual conversations that night. Use questions such as "What are you most concerned about this year?" "What is your child most looking forward to?" "Is there something I can do to make this year more fun/challenging/interesting for your child?" They will remember that you listened to them and appreciate you for it. Make a note of the parents and caregivers with whom you speak as the year progresses so that you can make sure you don't leave anyone out.

You might try to have three telephone or Zoom conversations each week with different families. You could have a brief conversation with the parent or caregiver volunteering in the school or on the playground. Conversations can take place in the basketball stands or during carpool. These conversations build relationships essential to forming the basis for a joyful parental community.

Besides having ongoing communication and conversations with parents, educators should consider involving parents in the school day in ways other than supervising lunch or overseeing the field trip. While these efforts are wonderful ways of engaging parents and guardians in their child's school, they are not available opportunities for everyone. As part of building relationships with students and their families, find out what work the parent/caregiver does and invite them in to speak about it. It doesn't matter what the job is—students are interested in the adult world of work and would love to hear a brief presentation on any parent's job. Also, some parents have skills at sewing, designing, inventing, experimenting, showing or teaching that students appreciate. Invite those parents into your classroom. Once you have them there, you can build a relationship that will serve you well as you work with them to assure the success of their children.

Many teachers realize the value of the assignment notebook or planner as a tool for communication. If students are required to write in their planner a sentence summarizing what happened in class, they not only have a memory-jog as they start their homework, but they also have information for a parent perusing the planner. We all know that young people can be totally non-communicative when it comes to talking about school, particularly as they advance in grade levels. A vague question such as, "What'd you do in school today?" is generally met by, "Nothing," or "Why?" (or, if they remember, "Bob threw up."). Planners help parents ask more direct questions: "It says here you saw a movie in science class, what was it about?" "What did your teacher say today about the civil rights movement?" "When is this Spanish skit due?"

The important thing to remember is that our lives and the lives of our students are better served if we can involve their parents in positive relationships. It's hard to dislike someone who genuinely likes your child, so perhaps we need to do a better job of communicating what it is we do like about our students to their parents. Building the relationships with honest, affirming comments about their offspring goes a long way to helping parents listen when we have to offer news that is not so great or advice that is hard to hear. Both types of communication are sometimes necessary in working for the benefit of the student.

ENGAGING IN HARD CONVERSATIONS WITH PARENTS

Currently, we are dealing with seemingly irreconcilable differences on many issues. We must recognize that diversity exists *within* groups as much as *between* groups. When dealing with polarizing topics, how do we decide whether to stand our ground or seek common ground? In the opinion piece "A Guide to Diffusing

Charged Conversations With Parents," Irshad Manji says we need to replace the "either/or" paradigm with the "both/and" lens. She points out that standing one's ground is about *what* we believe. Seeking common ground is about *how* we express what we believe. Therefore, we should stand our ground *and* seek common ground. "America needs truth and reconciliation. None of us has a monopoly on the former. Achieving the latter will require moral courage—the ability to remind our ego that listening is not losing" (Manji, 2021).

A dynamic opportunity for having a conversation and building relationships is the parent conference. Conversations with parents reinforce both parties' concern for the student and a mutual willingness to act as resources going forward. Involving parents in our goal to provide a challenging, engaging, caring, safe environment for students only makes sense. They are a huge part of the success equation for their kids, and they are an integral part of how joyful our teaching experience is. Several of the ideas we provided for relationship building among adults at school can also be applied to parents and guardians.

Cort (2022) offers these ideas for creating a parent–teacher relationship that benefits our kids:

1. We embrace that we get to co-create and decide what kind of relationship we want to have. We ask, "Do we want to be a community of people who complain about each other? Or do we want to be a community who works together toward our shared goals?"

2. From this shared understanding, we assume the best in each other, communicating directly rather than talking about each other with others.

3. We support each other, genuinely asking how we can best meet our shared goals. We co-construct the plan to meet as many of our goals as possible. When we are confused or challenged, we ask how to clear up the confusion or meet the challenge. Simply put, we resist assuming the other is not fulfilling the role of caregiver or teacher. (pp. 69–70)

STUDENT-LED CONFERENCES

While we definitely want teachers to have significant conversations with parents, we also think it is our job to help parents have meaningful conversations with their children. Student-led conferences (SLCs) force students to set their own goals and outline their plans to meet those goals.

SLCs are something that all grade levels and schools should seriously consider. They help build a better relationship between teachers and students and between students and parents. They give more ownership and more responsibility to the student and give them an opportunity to have a voice in their education. Tips for effective SLCs can be found in Appendix 8.1.

Action Step 8.1

EMPOWERING STUDENT-LED CONFERENCES

Scan QR Code 8.1 to watch the 5-minute video, *Student-Led Conferences: Empowerment and Ownership.* The students in this video attend a magnet school. How do you think SLCs at your school would compare to the ones in this film? How could SLCs help empower your students to share responsibility for their learning?

LEARNING TOURS

Shanna Speakman-Spickard (2018), writes that she and her administrative team at Milan Middle School set up learning tours for parents that include a presentation on goals and practices, five three-minute classroom walkthroughs, and a building tour. Her team invites parents on their email list and advertises the event on social media. They start the morning with coffee, pastries, and conversation. A brief icebreaker helps the team familiarize themselves with the parents' learning expectations. Though groups were small in the beginning, the school is hoping to build on their initial success as they continue the tours once a quarter. Speakman-Spickard believes the learning tours engage parents and provide ambassadors for promoting the positive aspects of their schools.

The Community—"It Takes a Village"

Okay, we're a little tired of that "takes a village" slogan, too, but there is a certain truth to it. Successful schools can help build positive communities, and likewise, healthy, thriving communities can help influence positive schools. Even though parents and guardians are part of the larger community in which your school functions, statistically it is likely that fewer than 30 percent of the households in your community have a child in school. As a result, most the adults in your area have no clue what is happening there.

The same Gallup Poll we mentioned earlier showed (as it has every year the poll has been taken) that most parents/guardians give their child's school a "B" rating. More than two thirds of parents are okay with what's happening in their child's school. Why then, does education get such a bad reputation? One reason is the media portrays schools as dangerous and ineffective. In other words, the families of the students you teach are generally satisfied with what is happening at your school—it's *those other schools* that are in trouble. For community members who have no children in school, you are *those other schools*. A second reason teachers and education are misunderstood is that the public doesn't know what is happening in schools these days, and we don't take time to tell them.

Where does your general community, most of whom do not have children in school, get their information? For a majority of them, they rely on the local media. We are all aware that newspapers, radio, TV, podcasts, internet sites, and so forth are supported by advertising, and the point is to generate more visits to increase ad revenue. It would seem that bad news sells more than good news because media outlets certainly print, show, and talk about more of the startling, bizarre, unsavory, murderous, and fantastic than they do the warm, generous, and caring. In other words, school shootings and bullying make better news than students happily engaging in everyday reading, writing, and all kinds of great learning activities.

Many adults not involved in education believe that schools aren't doing their job anymore. They have been told that schools do not teach handwriting or the right kind of math. They hear horror stories about what kinds of books teachers are reading to their students. They think teachers don't care. They think students are not being prepared as well as students in other countries. All this habitual skepticism results in a strong opposing force that works against our movement toward optimism.

CONNECTING OUR CLASSROOMS TO THE COMMUNITY

So perhaps it is time for we the teachers to educate the public about what is happening in our schools. See if you can find out how much your district spends on advertising or public relations each year. Most school districts spend nothing or next to nothing because they don't have to advertise to get kids to come to their school. It's a state requirement. But district administrators forget that a considerable number of taxpayers in their district have no idea what is happening in their local schools. Superintendents often don't focus on this disconnect until it is time to pass a bond issue or levy a new tax.

Tips for Engaging Parents

In her presentation, "Three C's for Parent Engagement," Judith Baenen offers these ideas:

1. If there is a bank within your district boundaries, go visit with the bank manager. The higher up in position in the bank (it'd be great if you could visit with the president) the better. Many banks have a requirement or at least a desire to serve the needs of the community in some way. They can help the school (no cost involved) by allowing you to display schoolwork in the lobby. You will assure them it will be attractive and appropriate. Then go back to school and mat everyday work, lab reports, math assignments, social studies homework, etc. and arrange an exhibit for the bank lobby. Everyday work is the key—too often schools exhibit artwork or special poetry units. The ordinary taxpayer wants to see "schoolwork." When they enter the lobby of the bank, they will say things like, "Gee—this math looks hard. Wow, look what they're doing in sixth grade over at Lincoln School," or "Hmm, I didn't think they taught handwriting anymore—look at this from Carver Elementary."

    The bank can also occasionally allow you to use their electronic sign to advertise school successes like: "Our whole eighth grade read the *Diary of Anne Frank* last month" or "Our third graders have all mastered their multiplication timed test." Of course, if you have a band concert coming up, that can go there, too.

2. Another way of letting your community know what you are doing is to use your local eatery as a base for *advertising*. Here's how it works: You go to a nearby café or fast-food restaurant that uses placemats as part of the dining experience. It can be a chain or a local establishment. Talk to the manager. Offer to provide placemats for the restaurant for perhaps once each month. The advantage for the restaurant is that your placemats will increase the number of customers and also be good for the local school (win–win, wouldn't you say?). Back at school, laminate students' everyday schoolwork to approximate placemat size. Be sure to put the name of the school someplace on the mat. Ask parents for permission to display their child's work at the local eatery.

    Families whose children's work is on a placemat will visit the eatery to see them and be proud and perhaps invite aunts, uncles, cousins, and neighbors, thereby increasing customers. Other customers will be exposed to everyday scholarship from your school. This idea can also be used for laminating or screening student work onto grocery bags for use at the nearby supermarket or store.

3. Of course, students are the best representatives of the school and offer a remarkable reality to taxpayers who believe all the negativity they read and hear from the media. Go to your local mall, shopping area, or grocery store. For this project you need a long table, three to four students and an adult to supervise. This activity can be done once a month or more—check with the manager.

(Continued)

(Continued)

Take the students, the table, and the supervisor to the desired location and set up the table in a well-trafficked area. Have the students bring their everyday work. Give them a bit of training about how to speak with adults. The supervisor hangs back. When shoppers come by, the role of the student is to say, "Excuse me, Ma'am. I'm from Lincoln School. Do you have a moment? I'd like to tell you what we're doing right now in math (science, social studies, technology, language arts, etc.)." The student then goes on to explain whatever is on his or her paper—any of which will likely blow the mind of the shopper. Later, that shopper will remember the child's politeness and intelligence—a credit to the school.

There are many ways to connect to the community and perhaps you have tried many or all of these. You can partner with local businesses, you can invite in speakers, you can engage students in civic activities and clean-up projects. Keep at it—all of these activities enhance the joyfulness and optimism in the broader neighborhood in which you live. Often you will find support where you thought there was none, and you can bring that affirmation back to your classroom and shower it on the students.

Educators must, now more than ever, be prepared to step up and take a more forceful stand in promoting what they believe constitutes a quality education. They can no longer cede to politicians and business leaders the task of determining the purpose of an education, and then dictating it to educators, students, and the general public.

—Connolly (2013), educator, author

CONNECTING STUDENTS TO THE COMMUNITY

Several schools have embraced service learning and volunteer work as part of their curriculum. Using the project-based-learning (PBL) model, some middle schools and high schools require "capstone projects" that require students to solve a local issue or work within their community to make it a better place. Inspired educators work to provide academic success both inside and outside of the classroom. Sometimes, having the community see what tenth graders are like can help build support for you as an educator. It might even help pass local tax initiatives for your school. Here are a few reasons to allow students to use their voices in working within their community or on a project to solve local issues.

School/Community projects may have the following impact:

- Allow students to be seen as a vital part of their community.

- Help with creativity and problem solving.

- Build confidence for the student.

- Help the community see the educational skills and attributes that prepare students for college or the work force.

- Provide great PR for your school and your students.

- Highlight great things that students can accomplish.

- Give students a sense of voice and choice.

Action Step 8.2

CONNECTING STUDENTS TO THE COMMUNITY

Scan QR Code 8.2 to watch the 3-minute trailer to the movie *Schools That Change Communities*. Would it be possible for your students to be more active and visible in your school's community? Why or why not? List the people needed to start a project like one of those shown in the film.

CONNECTING TEACHERS TO THE COMMUNITY

We recently discovered a gem of a resource for ideas to build camaraderie among staff members as well as show appreciation for their hard work. Middle school principal Eckert (2022) wrote *School Transformation Through Teacher Appreciation*. Many of her suggested activities inspire community involvement.

Community Scavenger Hunts and Goosechase

Kathleen Eckert

"Prior to the in-service day, hit up local businesses and restaurants to garner support for your school through coupons, gift certificates, and free trinkets. When teacher[s] enter the school building, use a deck of playing cars to divide your teachers into teams and send them on a wild goose chase through the local community. Each team will get in a car, drive to a different location, and then follow the clues by scanning QR codes at local businesses and restaurants. The first team that completes the scavenger hunt and makes it back to school without getting a ticket or having a wreck wins a prize! If anyone on your staff is competitive, this will be the one of their most memorable training days ever. It also helps gain involvement from community partners and stakeholders who can be a valuable asset to your school for years to come" (pp. 71–72).

Goosechase brings scavenger hunts into the digital world, and they are a lot of fun. You are able to set up different types of tasks/ activities and assign how many points you want each activity to be worth. For the tasks/activities—as you create them, you designate if the participants need to upload a picture, answer a question, or be at certain GPS location. The first time we did a staff Goosechase during a professional development day, I designed it as a "learn your community" game. For instance, upload a picture of someone from your team taking shopping carts from the parking lot into the store or driving through an apartment complex where students live. This can be used as a fun game but also allows your staff to see where your students live.

A few years ago, our district moved to a feeder pattern system for our schools. To help build team unity between our campuses from elementary to high school, I created Goosechase. (When using Goosechase you can assign teams or have the participants pick teams.) For this one, I chose to assign teams that were composed of two elementary school teachers, one middle school teacher, and one high school teacher. Each team was assigned a shape and color. For instance, orange circle or purple triangle. All schools met in the high school auditorium. Hillwood Middle School teachers were given a sign to hold up for their assigned groups so that elementary and high school teachers could easily meet their assigned groups.

Then I decided to also incorporate various community members who I partner with during the school year. My thought was I would expose the community members to a larger audience base, and it would be a way of thanking that community member. For instance, we have a close partnership with The Spurrier Group Realtors, so one of the tasks was to go to a location where they were set up and take a business card.

Some tasks incorporated various people from our school district and school locations. One of the most popular tasks was to take a selfie with your whole team and the superintendent. I had told him to hide and put out random tweet clues about his location. This task was worth the most points.

As part of this Goosechase, we gave them a Twitter challenge. Our superintendent is a huge Twitter person, so at the end of the Goosechase, I had him give out the prizes. He told the participants they were trending number six in DFW with our hashtag. That means a lot of people got to see our staff bonding and having fun in the community (p. 72).

CONNECTING THE COMMUNITY
THROUGH SOCIAL MEDIA

Building on the idea of a Twitter challenge, schools across the country are starting to brand themselves with hashtags so that positive messages and stories reach students, parents/caregivers, teachers, administrators, community members, and anyone with an interest in their school. Posting event pictures, sharing inspiring stores, and reporting on upbeat classroom activities can be done by students, teachers, parent ambassadors, administrators, or anyone interested in keeping the community informed about what is right about education in their area. The school can create a special task force of individuals from students to parent ambassadors to make sure the hashtag posts are current and informative. Clubs can appoint different members to be responsible for putting up weekly posts with the school hashtag, and everyone can be asked to help monitor that tweets remain affirming.

Activating Our Power

As we have said repeatedly in this book, it is time for teachers to take back our power. The important thing to remember in all of this is that you are not in it alone. By careful listening, keeping an open attitude, and doing a little Nancy Drew-like sleuthing, you can discover others on your team and in your building who want the same things for the students and the school that you do. There are teachers, support staff, and administrators who are working for the same goals. Additionally, the families of the students you teach provide wide avenues of support. Indeed, the community at large understands that a thriving local school is in everyone's best interest.

Maybe this means that you may have to become a bit *political.* Once you discover (through hearsay or obvious action) other teachers who share your attitude toward school and education, approach them openly to form an informal caucus. This caucus can do the following:

- Tactfully share ideas with the school teams and administration

- Take action to implement the ideas

- Build a network to find other like-minded individuals

- Speak up about larger issues affecting educators and students

- Inspire and support educators to run for office, serve on policy-making boards, write letters, create podcasts, maintain an active blog

- Provide a support system when we inevitably stumble or miscue

Your caucus will attract both positive and negative attention, but that's fine. We need to get things out in the open and commence the candid discussions. In doing that, you will find other colleagues who will become part of your action. At least you will be **doing something positive** toward your goal, and that is one of the steps in the Principles of Deliberate Optimism.

Telling Our Stories

A vast majority of our power is the track record of what we have already done for our students. There are few veteran teachers who cannot recall at least one student's life they significantly changed. For most of us, the list of lives we have impacted in a positive way would be quite lengthy. And yet, when is the last time you went into a teachers' lounge and heard someone say, "I think I changed a life today," "I think I made a difference," or even "I just ran into a young lady I taught twelve years ago, and you know what she said?"

We educators are generally givers who don't want to put ourselves in the limelight. We don't like to appear boastful or self-serving, so we say little about what we do, what we give, and what we give up to do our jobs. It is time for we-the-teachers to speak up. In an era where just about everyone in this world thinks they are an expert on school (just because they went to one), it is imperative that those on the frontlines find our collective voice and exercise it.

We should better communicate to our critics that teaching is a craft that must be honed over time. Much of what teachers do to optimize our time with students is invisible to the public eye. And how can we fault our detractors for not knowing about what all we do if we don't tell them?

Educators need to speak out to community groups, the media, and others who influence public opinion to let them know that we want to be accountable but that many aspects of the positive things we do every single day cannot be measured on a single standardized test. As teachers, we plant and sow seeds every day that may not blossom or fully flourish until long after our students have left our classrooms. But the lack of closure does not prevent us from going into our classrooms every day to try and reach every single child. We do it for one reason. We believe it's the right thing to do.

We believe we are making this world a better place and what we do matters. Despite the many paths we took to become teachers, our choice to remain in this profession is generally an act of deliberate optimism, and we need to do everything we can to reclaim the joy in education.

What is most needed for reclaiming our joy in education is that until proven otherwise, each of us needs to assume the best intentions in everyone else. Grace, forgiveness, and patience will take us where we need to go next. Granted, this business of shaping little humans for the future is indeed challenging. So okay then, let's *deal with it!*

••• DISCUSSION QUESTIONS AND ACTION STEPS

1. How important is salary in hiring and maintaining good teachers? Why do you think that is true? Do other teachers in general agree with your opinion? What about people outside the teaching profession—do they agree with you? Why or why not?

2. Discuss Dina Strasser's list of ways administrators can support teachers. Do you agree with the ones she stated? Did she leave out any that you would like to add?

3. Make a list of ways you think communication can be improved at your school. Prioritize the list by what you think would have the most immediate and greatest impact on morale. Would you or your caucus be willing to share your list with your school leaders? Why or why not?

4. Teachers often complain they are not being treated like professionals. What do they mean by that? How can teachers go about getting that changed?

5. Without violating privacy issues, how can administrators be more transparent in the way they run the school? Are there times that teachers just need to trust their administrators to do the right thing without questioning them? Explain your answer.

6. Do you agree with the authors' assertion that parental involvement is strengthened by parent/educator conversations? Explain.

7. List some of the ways you have reached out to parents in the past. How successful were your attempts? Is there something you would like to do that you haven't tried yet (or done for quite some time)? Explain.

(Continued)

(Continued)

8. If you already have student-led conferences at your school, discuss how they could be improved. If you have not yet implemented them, use the questions in Appendix 8.1 to explore how you could start using them.

9. What ideas can you add to the ones in the chapter for engaging the community with students at your school?

10. In your group, tell at least one story about a difference you made in a student's life. Have you told anyone else that story? Why or why not?

Action Steps for School Leaders

1. Whenever possible, arrange for outstanding teachers to present to community groups, such as the Chamber of Commerce, school board, Rotary Club, Lion's Club, and so forth, on what is happening at your school. Also make yourself available to local groups to answer questions or accompany students who are making a presentation.

2. Arrange informal parent meetings either at school or at a neutral location (local library, church meeting room, or even the laundromat) for parents with shared interests. If you have non-English-speaking parents, arrange to have a local pastor, a bilingual college student, or some other person who speaks their language to act as an interpreter.

3. Sometimes community members judge a school by its outward appearance. At least every two weeks walk around your school and make a detailed visual scan of your campus. Is the marquee sign updated? Are plants pruned and well cared for? Is the parking lot clean? Is the lawn mowed? Are the structures free of graffiti? Students, staff, and community members can be enlisted for a "grounds makeover," if one is needed. Provide tools, gloves, and food.

4. Work with a committee of staff members to ensure that your school is parent-friendly. Signs, posters, and other visuals should help visitors navigate your campus and feel welcome. Discuss with staff and students your expectations for how visitors to the campus will be treated. (You might even have a "secret visitor," much like a "secret shopper," who appears on campus and makes note of each person who is especially friendly or helpful. Those that are noted could receive a small gift card or just a thank you note from the committee.)

5. Reread Dina Strasser's list of ways administrators can support teachers. Give yourself a letter grade on how well you do on each of the five areas listed. Plan on how you will improve an area where your score could be better.

		GRADE YOURSELF	WHAT'S YOUR IMPROVEMENT PLAN?
1.	Equip Teachers		
2.	Communication and Transparency		
3.	Trust Teachers		
4.	Advocate for Teachers		
5.	Respect and Empower Teachers		

6. On your school website, include a place for staff members, students, parents, and community members to post suggestions for making your school a better place. Allow the posts to be anonymous, if desired, but you will want to screen all posts privately. Select appropriate comments and questions and respond to them on the website. It is a great way for you to address issues of concerned individuals, to get novel ideas, and to be aware of brewing problems.

7. Create a parent lounge/workroom where parents can meet, create study materials for their children, and relax between volunteer assignments. Get parents to oversee the room, coordinate workshops and informal meetings for themselves, and run the volunteer program for your school. Visit often and make a regular "state of our school" presentation and answer any questions they may have.

8. Use the parent portal to its full extent. You can never over-communicate. Find out each family's preferred mode of communication (do not assume each house has a computer or even a phone). Share this information with all staff.

9. Make sure that student photos and student work is visible immediately upon entering your building. Let families and visitors know that students are what your school is all about. If you can't paint over the mural from the class of 1991, find another wall for the current class's work.

10. Invite policy makers and community members into your school. Tell them to shadow an educator for just one day. Assure them they will see the best use of tax dollars they have ever witnessed.

APPENDICES

Appendix I.1: Life Orientation Test

Developed by psychologists Michael Scheier and Charles Carver

To gauge your optimism level with this test, indicate your response to each item that follows:

A—strongly agree; B—agree; C—feel neutral; D—disagree; E—strongly disagree

(Don't let your answer to one question influence another.)

_____ 1. In uncertain times, I usually expect the best.

_____ 2. It's easy for me to relax.

_____ 3. If something can go wrong for me, it will.

_____ 4. I'm always optimistic about my future.

_____ 5. I enjoy my friends a lot.

_____ 6. It's important for me to keep busy.

_____ 7. I hardly ever expect things to go my way.

_____ 8. I don't get upset too easily.

_____ 9. I rarely count on good things happening to me.

_____ 10. Overall, I expect more good things to happen to me than bad.

Ignore your answers to items 2, 5, 6, and 8. Those are fillers.

Subtotal your scores for items 1, 4, and 10 as follows: A is 4 points; B—3; C—2; D—1; E—0.

Subtotal your scores for items 3, 7, and 9 as follows: A is 0 points; B—1; C—2; D—3; E—4.

Add those subtotals for an overall optimism score.

The range is from 0 to 24, from extreme pessimism to extreme optimism, with virtual neutrality being the midpoint, 12.

Most people who have taken the test are slightly optimistic, Carver said. For instance, among 2,000 college students, the average score was 14, with two-thirds scoring between 10 and 18.

Appendix I.2: Happiness and Optimism Tests

To get a sense of just how optimistic you are, you can take one or more of the following surveys online:

Psychology Today Happiness Test

http://psychologytoday.tests.psychtests.com/take_test
.php?idRegTest=1320

About.com Optimism Test

http://stress.about.com/library/optimismquiz/
bl_15optimism_quiz.htm

Los Angeles Times Optimism Test

http://articles.latimes.com/2000/jan/05/news/mn-50931

Appendix I.3: Life on a Roll

Purpose: To have teachers reflect on why they became teachers and what events brought them to their current positions.

Materials needed

Pencils, pens, markers

Rulers

Rolls of paper (similar to receipt machine tape)

Procedure

1. Give each teacher a long strip of paper. Have her mark off a timeline of her life from beginning to present.

2. Ask each teacher to chronologically note important events in his life (good and bad), including those that influenced his choice to become a teacher.

3. Allow teachers plenty of time to create their timelines, draw pictures, write words, or otherwise depict their information in a way that best suits them.

4. Tell teachers they do not have to share personal events if they don't want to but they should mark the proper place on their timelines with a code of some sort to indicate to them when it happened.

5. Either with a partner or in small groups have participants share their timelines (as much as they are comfortable with) and explain how they ended up where they are now.

(Optional): You can display the timelines for others to see (with or without names on them).

Appendix 1.1: Four Principles of Deliberate Optimism

1. Gather information.
2. Control what you can.
3. Do positive things.
4. Own your part.

Appendix 1.2: Four Principles of Deliberate Optimism

WORKSHEET

1. What is the challenge you are dealing with? Explain fully the situation you have and how you feel about what is happening.

2. What steps have you taken to gather as much information as you can about your situation? Where can you go to find further facts and evidence?

3. List the contributing factors that are beyond your control at this time. Explain how you can minimize their impact on your present situation.

4. List all the things you *could* control that would make a positive impact on your situation.

5. Describe the things you are willing to do currently to improve your situation. Be specific.

6. What steps could you take but do not plan to take at this time? Explain why you are choosing not to control some of the variables that you could.

7. What will be your first step toward improving your situation? When will you do it? Estimate the time it will take you to put your plan into action.

8. When will you review your progress toward your goal? What indicators will you look for in order to know if you are successful or not?

Appendix 1.3: Realistic Awareness

(CHECKING THE FACTS)

Before acting or reacting to news about a challenge or problem, it is helpful to answer the following questions about the information you have.

Describe the mandate, problem, event, or proposal:

_____

_____

_____

1. If the report is about what "they" are doing, who exactly are "they"? Who is responsible for the decision and/or decision implementation? Be as specific as possible.

_____

_____

_____

2. Have I fact-checked the information I have? How thorough was I? How could I learn more?

_____

_____

_____

3. Have I heard more than one side of the issue? Did I give equal weight to differing views? If not, why?

_____

_____

_____

4. Is my conclusion or opinion based on the views of others? Have I considered their possible bias(es) and credibility? Are there limiting factors to accepting their views at face value? What are they?

_____

_____

_____

5. Is it possible my opinion was shaped by my preexisting ideas and conclusions? Did I attribute motives to people's words and/or actions based on my prior beliefs? How fair was I in my judgments?

_____

_____

_____

6. Was there an opportunity for me to give my opinion or to contribute my ideas that I failed to capitalize on?

_____

_____

_____

7. Am I more focused on reacting to the news about this situation than on figuring out a way to make it work? Explain.

_____

_____

_____

8. Have I closely examined any supporting data and taken a hard look at their rationale?

_____

_____

_____

9. Have I made an effort to contact other schools or groups who have tried similar ideas?

_____

_____

_____

10. Have I reflected on the full potential of this idea (both pros and cons) with a concentration on how it will affect students?

_____

_____

_____

Appendix 1.4: Recognizing and Celebrating Staff

Pam Koutrakos

LEARN ABOUT IDENTITIES, INTERESTS, AND ASSETS

- Ask! Conversations, surveys, interest inventories
- Take part in building activities (breakfast clubs, afterschool events)
- Attend committee meetings and grade-level/department meetings
- Jot observed assets during classroom visits
- Transform building walkthroughs into celebration walks

HONOR, IDENTITIES, INTERESTS, AND ASSETS

- Offer choice through collaboration menus
- Use observed assets to create goals and learning plans
- Co-design coaching cycles and residencies
- Offer personalized study groups
- Expand options for professional text study
    - book clubs, blog clubs, video clubs, lab site clubs, podcast clubs
    - weekly walk and talks, virtual meet-ups, in-person gatherings, coffee house excursions

Koutrakos, P. (2022). *Community-centered instructional coaching.* MiddleWeb. https://www.middleweb.com/47354/community-centered-instructional-coaching/

Appendix 3.1: Tips for Writing Letters to Students

- Write things that are positive and specific to the individual student. (Some students will compare their messages from you to see if you say the same things to everyone.)

- Make sure everyone gets at least one note from you during the year.

- Be truthful and be sincere. You can even be funny if that's how you interact with students, but be very careful that your words cannot be misinterpreted as sarcastic or negative (humor is tricky without the facial expressions and vocal tone to indicate that you are joking).

- Make sure your positive comments have "no strings attached."

- Don't make a big deal of presenting the note. Be as private as possible (you can even leave it in a locker or mail it).

- Don't ask them if they read it; give it freely, and let it go.

- Don't ask for or expect anything in return.

Source: Silver (2010, p. 42). Reprinted with permission of the publisher, Incentive Publications by World Book, World Book, Inc., all rights reserved.

Appendix 5.1: Some Simple Suggestions for Managing Stress

TWELVE STEPS TO REDUCE STRESS

1. TALK TO SOMEONE. Confide your worry to some levelheaded person you can trust—spouse, parent, friend, clergyman, family doctor, teacher, school counselor. Talking things out often helps you to see things in a clearer light and helps you see what you can do about it.

2. BE HONEST IN IDENTIFYING THE REAL SOURCE OF STRESS. Eliminate the source if possible. At least decide on a plan to keep it from getting the best of you.

3. ACCEPT WHAT YOU CAN'T CONTROL. Death and taxes are just a few of the things in life you can't avoid. Try to prepare for them as much as possible.

4. TAKE GOOD CARE OF YOURSELF. Eat right. Get enough sleep. Exercise. Learn a relaxation technique. Schedule recreation where you do something for pleasure, something that helps you forget about your work.

5. GO EASY ON YOUR CRITICISM. Don't expect so much of others, and you won't be disappointed. Instead, look for the good in others; you will feel better about yourself.

6. SHUN THE "SUPERWOMAN" or "SUPERMAN" URGE. Don't expect so much of yourself. Nobody is perfect or capable of doing everything. Decide what you can do well and what you like to do and put your effort into those things.

7. DO SOMETHING NICE FOR SOMEBODY ELSE. Then give yourself a pat on the back.

8. TAKE ONE THING AT A TIME. Attack the most urgent task first. Don't overestimate the importance of non-urgent tasks. Your mental and physical health are vitally important.

9. ESCAPE FOR A WHILE. Making yourself "stand there and suffer" is self-punishment and not a way to solve a problem. Recover your breath and balance but be prepared to deal with your difficulty when you are composed.

10. WORK OFF YOUR ANGER. If you feel like lashing out at someone, try holding off that impulse for a while. Do something constructive with that energy. Cool down, then handle the problem.

11. GIVE IN OCCASIONALLY. No one is right all of the time. And even if you are right, it is easier on the system to give in once in a while.

12. IF YOU NEED HELP, GET AN EXPERT. These simple suggestions may not be enough to help you handle your stress. If emotional problems become so distressing that you can't cope, you need PROFESSIONAL TREATMENT, just as you would for any other illness.

Appendix 6.1: Ten Tips for Improving Interpersonal Relationships

By Debbie Silver

1. Before you say anything to anyone, ask yourself three things:
   - Is it true?
   - Is it kind?
   - Is it necessary?

2. When people are talking to you, face them and give them your FULL attention. Put aside anything that is distracting you (mobile devices, paperwork, etc.), and concentrate on understanding what they are saying.

3. When people are talking to you, think about understanding what they are saying rather than what you want to reply. Just "taking turns talking" does not lead to healthy communication.

4. If you hear something negative about yourself, consider if there is any truth to it. If there is, fix it. If there isn't, ignore it and trust that the way you live your life will speak for itself.

5. When dealing with a tense conversation, lower your pitch, reduce your volume, and slow the rate of your speech. Remember the adage, "A soft answer turneth away wrath."

6. Refrain from using references to past behaviors to bolster your arguments. As much as possible, focus on "the here and now."

7. Remember that it is okay to "agree to disagree." People can strongly disagree on issues but maintain a healthy respect for each other as individuals.

8. Be honest, be specific, and as much as possible, be affirming to others. Never miss an opportunity to let someone know what it is you like about them.

9. Remember that laughter is the great equalizer. Always try to maintain a sense of humor about the foibles of other humans.

10. "Do not seek so much to be consoled, as to console; do not seek so much to be understood, as to understand; do not seek so much to be loved, as to love" (Prayer of St. Francis).

Appendix 6.2: Life Is a Theatre

Life is a theater . . . invite your audience carefully.

Not everyone is good enough to have a front row seat in our lives.

There are some people in your life who need to be loved from a distance.

It's amazing what you can accomplish when you let go of draining, negative relationships.

Observe the relationships around you. Which ones lift . . . which ones lean?

Which ones encourage . . . which ones discourage?

Which ones are on a path of growth uphill . . . which are going downhill?

When you leave certain people . . . do you feel better . . . or worse?

Which ones don't really understand or appreciate you?

The more you seek quality and growth, the easier it will become to decide who gets to sit in the **front row** . . . and who should be moved to the **balcony** of your life.

YOU **CANNOT** CHANGE THE PEOPLE **AROUND** YOU . . .

BUT YOU **CAN** CHANGE THE PEOPLE YOU ARE **AROUND**!

Choose wisely.

(Anonymous)

Appendix 7.1: Effective Team-Building Activities and Icebreakers

∙∙

COMMON ATTRIBUTES

Once participants are arranged in groups of four or five, ask one member to be the recorder and write down each individual's name. A group leader should help the members discover ten (hopefully unusual) things they have in common (e.g., We all have a pierced body part. Each of us has an addiction to chocolate. All of us drive red cars. Everyone's favorite TV show is *Survivor*.).

At the end of the ice breaker, one person from each group will introduce each group member and read their group's top five things they have in common. Groups can then vote on whom they thought did the best job of coming up with unusual common attributes. You can award a prize to the group with the most votes.

Pass out a sheet like this to each group.

List each group member's name:

_____

_____

_____

_____

_____

_____

List your most unusual things in common (they must be true and they must apply to ALL members of the group). When you are finished, put *stars* by your five favorite ones.

_____

_____

_____

_____

_____

_____

_____

MY NAME

In small groups, have each person make a name placard, introduce themselves, and tell what they know about why they have that particular name. Participants can talk about their first names, middle names, last names, or nicknames. We have seen some great conversations start with this activity. All kinds of insights are revealed about people's heritage, religion, family, and other seldom talked about topics.

WHAT I LIKE ABOUT YOU . . .

This is a powerful exercise in helping to build staff morale. Teachers trade papers and respond anonymously with written positive affirmations to colleagues. Often secondary teachers will grumble about doing this activity, but don't be surprised if some of them have a major attitude change after participating in this activity. It is worth the effort to make them do it.

Objective

To build a sense of belonging among staff members

Materials needed

Sheets of Paper

Step-by-step procedure

1. Tell the teachers that they are going to get the chance to receive affirmations in a very non-threatening method.

2. Ask each teacher to put their name at the top of a sheet of paper.

3. Collect all the papers and give these directions:

   - "I am going to pass out the papers randomly. When you receive someone's paper, think about that person and write something affirming to them. You must start your statement with the words 'I' or 'You.' You cannot use the words 'he' or 'she.'"

   - "When you finish with your message to the person listed at the top of the page, trade papers with someone. Make sure that you never give a paper to the person whose name is at the top. Trade with someone else if you need to."

   - "Please write something different from the other responses on the page. You can affirm the same attribute, but you must phrase it in a different way or give a different example."

   - "Keep trading until I call time."

4. Be sure to participate with the others on this activity. Put your sheet in there, too.

5. At the end of the activity, collect all papers.

6. Ask teachers to express how it felt to write positive affirmations to others. Why was it easier to write to some than to others? (Speak only in a general sense; do not name anyone specifically.)

7. Pass the papers back to their owners and allow participants to read what was written by their colleagues. Ask anyone who would like to share a particularly meaningful comment to do so.

PEOPLE BINGO

People Bingo is one of the most popular ice breakers because it's so easy to customize for your particular group and situation, and everyone knows how to play it. Make your own Bingo cards, or use one of the fabulous online card makers.

MAROONED

This icebreaker is a great introduction when people don't know each other, and it fosters team building in groups that already work together. Ask each participant to name the person, who is not a family member, that they would want to be stranded with on a deserted island and tell why.

IF I COULDN'T BE AN EDUCATOR

In small groups, ask teachers to finish the sentence, "If I could never be a teacher, I would probably want to be a ___." Group members take turns explaining what they would do for a career if they could not have any kind of a job in education and tell why.

Appendix 7.2: Student Accountability Sheet

Students can create their own guidelines on how to treat each other and hold each other responsible in class.

Expectation

As demonstrated by

Accountability

Here are examples of student-generated plans:

Expectation

Students will treat each other's property with respect.

As demonstrated by

If a student breaks something, takes something without permission, or harms someone else's possession

Accountability

Student must fix or replace the item. Student must write a letter of apology to the property's owner. Student must do a favor for the property owner.

Expectation

Students will act respectfully to each other in and out of class.

As demonstrated by

Taunting, harassing, name-calling, or threatening either in person, by written word, or through cyberspace

Accountability

Student will apologize in the same method he or she used to bully a classmate. Student will have a conference with the teacher. Student's parents may be notified about the incident.

Expectation

Students will not disrupt the learning process for others.

As demonstrated by

Talking out or over other people, doing something that distracts others, not sharing supplies or responsibilities

Accountability

Student will have a "time-out" to pay back the time he or she wasted. Student will have to apologize to the class. Student will have to help others regain any lost information or time they caused them.

Appendix 7.3: Loyalty

If you work for someone, then work for him: Speak well of him and stand by the institution he represents. Remember, an ounce of loyalty is worth a pound of cleverness. If you must growl, condemn, and eternally find fault, resign your position and when you are on the outside, complain to your hearts content. But as long as you are a part of the institution do not condemn it.

—Elbert Hubbard

Appendix 8.1: Student-Led Conferences

QUESTIONS TO ASK BEFORE YOU START

Here are some questions to ask before you venture down the path of student-led conferences. This activity can be used by an individual teacher, an entire team, or the whole staff.

1. What do we hope to accomplish by utilizing student-led conferences? What are our goals for the experience?

2. How can we align class time used for student preparation for student-led conferences with district/state standards and mandated curriculum?

3. What do we need to do to prepare ourselves to change from the traditional parent–teacher conferences to student-led conferences? What information and training will we need?

4. Are our students ready for student-led conferences? What training will our students need? How will we begin to get them ready for this next step?

5. How can we prepare our parents for the move to student-led conferences? How do we inform them throughout the process?

6. What types of work samples do we need to collect for the conferences?

7. What projects and demonstrations can the students present during the conference?

8. How can we include elective (encore) teachers in the new conference format?

9. Can we use technology to enhance the conferences and/or reach out to parents who are unable to physically be there?

10. How will we access how well we met our goals? How will we collect data from students and parents after the event?

Here are two good resources on student-led conferences that can provide you with more details and information:

- https://www.educationworld.com/a_admin/admin/admin112.shtml
- https://www.ascd.org/publications/educational_leadership/apr96/vol53/num07/When_Students_Lead_Parent-Teacher_Conferences.aspx

REFERENCES

Azzam, A. M. (2013). Handle with care. A conversation with Maya Angelou. *Educational Leadership, 71*(1), 10–13.

Baker, S. (2017, September 12). *The "whole school" approach: One principal devises a way to effectively handle disruptions.* https://www.scarymommy.com/addressing-behavioral-issues-classroom

Bandura, A. (1986). *Social foundations of thought and action: A social-cognitive theory.* Prentice Hall.

Bandura, A. (1989). Human agency in social cognitive theory. *American Psychologist, 44,* 1175–1184.

Bandura, A. (1997). *Self-efficacy: The exercise of control.* Worth Publishers.

Bandura, A. (2009). Cultivate self-efficacy for personal and organizational effectiveness. In E. A. Locke (Ed.), *Handbook of principles of organization behavior* (2nd ed., pp.179–200). Wiley.

Benac, E. (2017). *Gossip game ideas.* Our Pastimes. Retrieved from https://ourpastimes.com/gossip-game-ideas-8540539.html

Berckemeyer, J. C. (2012). *Taming of the team: How great teams work together.* Incentive by World Book.

Better Health Channel. (n.d.). *Mood and sleep.* https://www.betterhealth.vic.gov.au/health/healthyliving/Mood-and-sleep#sleep-and-moods

Blackburn, B. R. (2002). *Every teachers makes a difference—Every day.* MiddleWeb. https://www.middleweb.com/47640/every-teacher-makes-a-difference-every-day/

Brown, B. (2010). *The gifts or imperfection: Let go of who you think you're supposed to be and embrace who you are.* Hazelden Publishing.

Brown, B. (2013). *Daring greatly: How the courage to be vulnerable transforms the way we live, love, parent, and lead.* Gotham.

Cain, S. (2012). *Quiet: The power of introverts in a world that won't stop talking.* Crown Publishing.

Carlisle, G. (2022). *Teachers can positively impact education policy, we just have to use our teacher voice.* https://www.edsurge.com/news/2022-03-24-teachers-can-positively-impact-education-policy-we-just-have-to-use-our-teacher-voice

Cherry, K. (2022). *8 signs you are an introvert.* Verywell Mind. https://www.verywellmind.com/signs-you-are-an-introvert-2795427

Collaborative for Academic, Social, and Emotional Learning (CASEL). (2022). *What is the CASEL framework?* CASEL.org. https://casel.org/fundamentals-of-sel/what-is-the-casel-framework/#:~:text=A%20framework%20creates%20a%20foundation,advance%20students'%20learning%20and%20development

Collins, J. (2001). *Good to great.* Harper Collins.

Connolly, M. R. (2013). *Educators must be prepared to challenge politicians and business leaders' education agenda.* http://michaelrconnollyjr.weebly.com/1/post/2013/05/educators-must-be-prepared-to-challenge-politicians-and-business-leaders-education-agenda.html

Connors, N. A. (2000). *If you don't feed the teacher they eat the students: Guide to success for administrators and teachers.* Incentive Publications.

Cort, J. (2022). *Help us begin: HUB strategies and mindsets for meaningful conversations with kids, especially when you are challenged by the topic.* Association for Middle Level Education.

Crum, A. J., & Langer, E. J. (2007). Mindset matters: Exercise and the placebo effect. *Psychological Science, 18*(2), 165–171.

Curwin, R. (2013). *Cynicism is contagious; so is hope.* Eutopia. http://www.edutopia.org/blog/cynicism-is-contagious-richard-curwin

Deci, E. L., & Ryan, R. M. (2000). The "what" and "why" of goal pursuits: Human needs and the self-determination of behavior. *Psychological Inquiry, 11*, 227–268.

DeMatthews, D. E., & Su-Keene, J. S. (2022). *Rx for principals: Take in joy.* EducationWeek. https://www.edweek.org/leadership/opinion-rx-for-principals-take-in-the-joy/2022/03

DeWitt, P. M. (2022). *De-implementation: Creating the space to focus on what works.* Corwin Press.

DiTullio, G. (2022). *Bringing teachers into instructional leadership teams.* Edutopia. https://www.edutopia.org/article/bringing-teachers-instructional-leadership-teams?utm_content=linkpos1&utm_source=edu-legacy&utm_medium=email&utm_campaign=weekly-2022-08-31

Eckert, K. (2022). *School transformation through teacher appreciation.*

Elden, R. (2011). *See me after class: Advice for teachers by teachers* (2nd ed.). Sourcebooks.

Esquith, R. (2014). Can't wait for Monday. *Educational Leadership, 71*(5), 20–22.

Farber, K. (2022). *Stress, hypervigilance, and decision fatigue: Teaching during omicron.* EducationWeek. https://www.edweek.org/teaching-learning/opinion-stress-hypervigilance-and-decision-fatigue-teaching-during-omicron/2022/01

Ferlazzo, L. (2013). *Response: Recover from bad days by seeing "disasters as opportunities."* Education Week. https://www.edweek.org/teaching-learning/opinion-response-recover-from-bad-days-by-seeing-disasters-as-opportunities/2013/11

Frankl, V. (1946). *Man's search for meaning.* Beacon Press.

GALLUP. (2013). *Gallup poll on education.* www.gallup.com

Gaskell, M. (2022). *How to quiet the hyperactive hive mind in schools.* Tech & Learning. https://www.techlearning.com/how-to/how-to-quiet-the-hyperactive-hive-mind-in-schools#:~:text=Using%20on%20and%20offline%20tools,in%20turn%2C%20individually%20harmful%20impacts

Goodman, J. *The humor project.* www.HumorProject.com

Gregorc, A. F. (1982). *An adult's guide to style.* Gregorc Associates.

Gregorc, A. F. (1984). Style as a symptom: A phenomenological perspective. *Theory into Practice, 23*(1), 51–55.

Gregorc, A. F. (n.d.). *Mind styles.* Retrieved October 2022, from http://www.web.cortland.edu/andersmd/learning/gregorc.htm

Hall, K. M. (2021). *How does lack of sleep affect your sex life?* GoodRX Health. https://www.goodrx.com/conditions/low-libido/how-lack-of-sleep-impacts-sex-life-libido-fertility

Hallowell, E. (2007). *Crazy busy.* Ballantine Books.

Hargreaves, A., & Fullan, M. (2013). The power of professional capital: With an investment in collaboration, teachers become nation builders. *Journal of Staff Development (JSD), 34*(3), 36–39. https://www.learningforward.org

Henderson, N. (2013). Havens of resilience. *Educational Leadership, 71*(1), 22–27.

Heubeck, E. (2022). *The stay interview: How it can help schools hold onto valued staff.* EducationWeek. https://www.edweek.org/leadership/the-stay-interview-how-it-can-help-schools-hold-onto-valued-staff/2022/06

Johnson, S. M. (2019). *Where teachers thrive: Organizing schools for success.* The President and Fellows at Harvard College.

Justworks. (2020). *12 tips for constructive criticism & peer feedback.* https://www.justworks.com/blog/dont-make-peer-to-peer-constructive-criticism-awkward

Kabat-Zinn, J. (2017). *Defining mindfulness.* Mindful Direct. https://www.mindful.org/jon-kabat-zinn-defining-mindfulness/

Kajitani, A. (2016). *The #1 factor that determines a toxic or thriving school culture.* EducationWeek. https://www.edweek.org/leadership/opinion-the-1-factor-that-determines-a-toxic-or-thriving-school-culture/2016/04#:~:text=Here's%20what%20I've%20concluded,students%20learn%20to%20get%20along

Klein, J. (2022). *What educators need: Building cultures of trust in an era of top-down educational legislation, getting smart.* https://www.gettingsmart.com/2022/08/04/what-educators-need-building-cultures-of-trust-in-an-era-of-top-down-educational-legislation/

Koutrakos, P. (2022). *Community-centered instructional coaching.* MiddleWeb. https://www.middleweb.com/47354/community-cen tered-instructional-coaching/

Larkin, D. B. (2013). 10 things to know about mentoring student teachers. *Phi Delta Kappan, 49*(7), 28–43.

Lee, D. (2022). *How schools can build a culture of support for educator mental health.* EdSurge. https://www.edsurge.com/news/2022 -04-29-how-schools-can-build-a-culture-of-support-for-edu cator-mental-health#:~:text=By%20increasing%20support%20 and%20creating,health%2C%20which%20can%20reduce%20stigma

Levin, S, Scott, C., Yang, M., Leung-Gagné, M., & Bradley, K. (2020). *Supporting a strong, stable principal workforce: What matter and what can be done.* ERIC. https://eric.ed.gov/?id=ED606481

Loewus, L. (2012, October 17). National Teacher of the Year: Give us a career path. *Education Week.* https://www.edweek.org/lead ership/opinion-national-teacher-of-the-year-give-us-a-career -path/2012/10

Mandela, N. (1995). *Long walk to freedom: Autobiography of Nelson Mandela.* Back Bay Books.

Manji, I. (2021). A *guide to diffusing charged conversations with parents.* EducationWeek. https://www.edweek.org/leader ship/opinion-a-guide-to-diffusing-charged-conversations-with -parents/2021/11

Marken, S., & Agrawal, S. (2022, June 13). *K–12 workers have highest burnout rate in U.S.* Gallup. https://news.gallup.com/ poll/393500/workers-highest-burnout-rate.aspx

Mason, J. (2021). Are teachers ok? No, and toxic positivity isn't helping. *We Are Teachers.* https://www.weareteachers.com/ toxic-positivity-schools/

Meade, L. (2022). *A principal's assessment: "We're not ok."* https:// www.edweek.org/leadership/opinion-principals-assessment -were-not-ok/2022/01

Merrimack College. (2022). *Merrimack College Teacher Survey.* https:// www.merrimack.edu/academics/education-and-social-policy/ about/merrimack-college-teacher-survey/

Mertz, J. (2013). *Building trust between generations—Six ways.* https://www.thindifference.com/2013/09/building-trust -generations-six-ways/

Morton, N. (2022, November 3). *In one giant classroom, four teaches manage 135 kids—and love it.* The Hechinger Report. https:// hechingerreport.org/in-one-giant-classroom-four-teachers -manage-135-kids-and-love-it/

Najarro, I. (2021). *Students aren't the only ones grieving.* EducationWeek. https://www.edweek.org/teaching-learning/students-arent-the -only-ones-grieving/2021/09

Nelson, S. (2013). *Teaching: The most noble profession.* http://www .huffingtonpost.com/steve-nelson/teaching-the-most-noble -p_b_2471894.html

Noddings, N. (2014). High morale in a good cause. *Educational Leadership, 71*(5), 15–18.

Paturel, A. (2022). *Sleep more, weigh less*. Web MD. https://www
.webmd.com/diet/sleep-and-weight-loss

Paz, I. G. (2022, January 24). Litter boxes for students who identify
as furries? Not so, says school official. *New York Times*. https://
www.nytimes.com/2022/01/23/us/politics/michigan-litter-box
-school.html

Peri, C. (2021). *What lack of sleep does to your mind*. WebMD. https://
www.webmd.com/sleep-disorders/features/emotions-cognitive

Pratt, E. (2019). *How sleep strengthen your immune system*.
Healthline. https://www.healthline.com/health-news/how-sleep
-bolsters-your-immune-system

Purdue University Global. (n.d.). *Generational differences in the workplace (Infographics)*. https://www.purdueglobal.edu/education
-partnerships/generational-workforce-differences-infographic/

Richardson, J. (2013). Wanted: Highly effective teachers. *Phi Delta
Kappan, 94*(7), 4.

Rockwell, D. (2013, February). 10 ways to "deal with" quiet people. *Leadership Freak Blog*. http://leadershipfreak.wordpress
.com/2013/02/05/10-ways-to-deal-with-quiet-people/

Rubenstein, J. S., Meyer, D. E., & Evans, J. E. (2001). Executive
control of cognitive processes in task switching. *Journal of
Experimental Psychology: Human Perception and Performance,
27*(4), 763–797.

Scheier M., Carver, C., & Bridges, M. W. (1994). Distinguishing optimism from neuroticism (and trait anxiety, self-mastery, and self-
esteem): A reevaluation of the Life Orientation Test. *Journal of
Personality and Social Psychology, 67*(6), 1063–1078.

School Retool. (2022). *Teacher-to-teacher feedback: Encourage teachers to educate each other*. https://schoolretool.org/big-idea/
teacher-to-teacher-feedback

Seligman, M. E. P. (2006). *Learned optimism: How to change your mind
and your life*. New Vintage Books.

Seligman, M. E. P., & Maier, S. F. (1967). Failure to escape traumatic
shock. *Journal of Experimental Psychology, 74*(1), 1–9.

SHRM. (2011). *Employee job satisfaction and engagement: A research
report*. https://www.shrm.org/hr-today/news/hr-magazine/
Documents/11-0618%20Job_Satisfaction_FNL.pdf

Silver, D. (2010). *Drumming to the beat of different marchers*. Incentive
by World Book.

Silver, D. (2013). Relax and recharge: 5 ways to de-stress this summer. *The Classroom Teacher 34*(2), 18.

Silver, D. (2021). *Fall down 7 times, get up 8: Raising and teaching
self-motivated learners, K–12* (rev. ed.). Corwin Press.

Silver, D. (2022). *Back to school—Level 8 of Jumanji?* AMLE website.
https://www.amle.org/back-to-school-level-8-of-jumanji/

Silver, D., & Stafford, D. (2017). *Teaching kids to thrive: Essential skills
for success*. Corwin Press.

Silver D., Berckemeryer, J. C., & Baenen, J. R. (2015). *Deliberate
optimism: Reclaiming the joy in education*. (1st ed.). Corwin Press.

Speakman-Spickard, S. (2018). *Take parents on a tour.* Principal. https://www.naesp.org/wp-content/uploads/2020/02/Speakman-Spickard_SO18.pdf

Strasser, D. (2014). An open letter on teacher morale. *Educational Leadership, 71*(5), 10–13.

Strasser, D. (2022). *Getting things done in your school district.* MiddleWeb. https://www.middleweb.com/46494/getting-things-done-in-your-school-district/

Suni, E. (2022). *How lack of sleep impacts cognitive performance and focus.* https://www.sleepfoundation.org/sleep-deprivation/lack-of-sleep-and-cognitive-impairment

Tate, M. (2022). *Healthy teachers, happy classrooms.* Solution Tree.

Van Dongen, H., Maisliln, G., Mullington, J. M., & Dinges, D. F. (2003). The cumulative cost of additional wakefulness: Dose-response effects on neurobehavioral function and sleep physiology from chronic sleep restriction and total sleep deprivation. *Sleep, 26*(2), 117–126.

Will, M. (2022). *Teaching is hard. Take a break, 'Abbott Elementary' stars urge teachers.* Education Week. https://www.edweek.org/teaching-learning/teaching-is-hard-take-a-break-abbott-elementary-stars-urge-teachers/2022/07

Will, M., & Superville, D. R. (2022). *Don't forget the adults: How school and districts can support educator mental health.* https://www.edweek.org/teaching-learning/dont-forget-the-adults-how-schools-and-districts-can-support-educator-mental-health/2022/03

Wolpert-Gawron, H. (2013). *Teachers: Staying positive in trying times.* Edutopia. http://www.edutopia.org/blog/teaching-staying-positive-trying-time-heather-wolpert-gawron

Workplace Bullying Institute (WBI). (2022). *Workplace Bullying.* https://workplacebullying.org/defined/

INDEX

A SAGE Publishing Company

Helping educators make the greatest impact

CORWIN HAS ONE MISSION: to enhance education through intentional professional learning.

We build long-term relationships with our authors, educators, clients, and associations who partner with us to develop and continuously improve the best evidence-based practices that establish and support lifelong learning.